D1385307

Saffola

PRESENTS

Sanjeev Kapoor's

# Khazana of Healthy Tasty Recipes

In association with Alyona Kapoor

**Saffola**
PRESENTS
**Sanjeev Kapoor's**

# Khazana of Healthy Tasty Recipes

In association with Alyona Kapoor

Nutritional information in association with Dr. Mrs. Sujata Udeshi (Ph. D.)
Food Scientist, Nutritionist, Dietitian

POPULAR PRAKASHAN

POPULAR PRAKASHAN PVT. LTD.
35-C, Pt. Madan Mohan Malaviya Marg
Tardeo, Mumbai-400 034.



First Published 2000
First Reprint February 2000
Second Reprint January 2002
Third Reprint February 2003
Fourth Reprint November 2003
Fifth Reprint October 2005

(3619)

ISBN - 81-7154-671-4

PRINTED IN INDIA
by Saurabh Printers Pvt. Ltd.,
A-16, Sector-IV, Noida 201301 and
Published by Ramdas Bhatkal
for Popular Prakashan Pvt. Ltd.
35-C, Pt. Madan Mohan Malaviya Marg
Tardeo, Mumbai-400 034.

# AUTHOR'S *Note*

I am overwhelmed by the response that my first book – *Khazana of Indian Recipes* received from food lovers and readers. It is difficult to express in words the gratitude with which I hold the readers who have given me encouragement and confidence to do something different. My objective has been to make Indian food popular with everyone – whether fighting fit or leading a normal healthy life or even those who have to face dietary restrictions for reasons of their health. This book has specifically been written keeping in view people who are health conscious and those who have to restrict their diet to certain specific food, which is essential for keeping them fit.

It is normally understood that healthy food is not tasty food. The moment we are told to follow a restricted diet, we have a vision of a diet, which will be devoid of taste and which is a compulsion. I would like to assure you that all food is healthy and that food cannot be tasteless. Every food item in itself has a taste of its own and contains certain vitamins and minerals. Similarly all oils have certain characteristics of their own, some are good for our health while some fats or oils may not be beneficial to health. However only a specialist can decide which type of oil suits a certain individual by understanding the metabolism of the body.

Healthy food would normally be defined as food that helps one keep in good health. It means that the food should have adequate quality nutrients. To maintain good health, it is imperative to keep an eye on what one eats and in what quantities. The emphasis on quantity is critical, because excess of anything can have adverse effect. It is important for people to consume food in proper quantities, however, the 'proper' amount for different people would definitely be different, depending on their age, physique and so on.

Different kinds of food, vegetables and fruits meet the daily requirement of various vitamins and minerals the body needs. However different body structures have different needs and hence each individual has to select his diet according to the demands of his body. The common notion about health food is that it is usually bland, insipid and tasteless. But it is not so. Food per se is healthy and tasty. Using less oil does not necessarily rob the food of its good taste, and on many occasions this can actually enhance the taste of food. When we use more oil, the food becomes oily and the predominant taste in the food is that of oil. Using less amount of oil can help to bring out the aroma of other ingredients, which could make it tastier and mouth watering.

The important aspect of food is its preparation. When we treat a child with love and affection and caress him, he responds well. The same is true for everything else, including food. If we prepare our food with love, affection and passion, there is no reason why it would not reach one's expectations. The more the time you devote to anything – your clothes, your physique, your mannerism, your education, your profession – and that too with enthusiasm, the better results you achieve. In the same way more time should be given to the understanding of food. More time does not mean that you only have to spend your time cooking, but that you should give it complete attention when you do.

In the book, to make matters easy, we have briefly talked about a few ingredients and the type of nutrients they contain. This way, you can choose those ingredients that contain the vitamins and minerals you require. Each recipe serves four and has been provided with essential nutritional information in terms of their actual values. One can easily browse through the book and make up one's mind about the taste that would match their nutritional needs.

I must add that while writing this book many people asked me if this is a LOW CALORIE recipe book. It makes me wonder if most people perceive Healthy food as food that is in only low in calories. I would like to assure you that through this book we are trying to redefine health food and we would need your feedback to make our mission a reality. I am a firm believer that one can easily cook, create and eat food that is not only healthy but tasty as well.

Happy Healthy and Tasty Living! (Do spend some quality time in regular exercise as well).

Eating healthy is fun. It is easy to cook and choose foods that would keep you and your family healthy. Healthy meals no longer need be boring and insipid, they can easily taste delicious. All you need is a little time to think about the food you and your family eat and to think positively about food and health. So if you decide that your family's diet could do with some improvement, the changes have to be worked out and implemented now.

Changing old habits is not very easy, but nor it is too difficult and the results are worth the effort. Any change needs some time and effort. It should start at an early age. Children in their formative years are easy to mould. The best gift we can give our children, is the appreciation of healthy food. This could be done by means of a practical example in every day eating and life style. This way they will not think of changing their habits later in life and will have the benefit of good foods all their lives.

A simple way to begin is to start with a few changes like replacing white bread with brown whole wheat bread, eating fruits and vegetables with their skin on. It is simple to achieve and definitely more nutritious.

Healthy eating does not mean eating less or more. Neither does it mean getting fanatic or cranky about certain foods. It means eating correctly and wisely, with understanding. It involves having a positive and holistic approach and attitude towards food.

The recipes and information in this book will make it easier for you to adopt healthy and tasty ways of eating. It also helps to understand and follow general guidelines of health and nutrition, while you dish out delectable meals for your family. The nutritional information provided in this book is of a generic nature. For any specific condition, it is best to take professional help or advise.

**Dietary and health guidelines:**

**1. Eat variety of foods in adequate amount**

* Fruits
* Vegetables
* Whole grain products
* Milk, curds, and other milk products
* Flesh foods, eggs, fish and poultry
* Pulses, legumes and dals

**2. Maintain desirable weight**

Being overweight increases the chances of developing some chronic diseases like diabetes and heart ailments and certain types of cancer. Obesity is also associated with high blood pressure, increased level of triglyceride and cholesterol. That is why it is important to try and maintain a desirable weight.

**To help control overeating and to lose weight:**

* Eat slowly and take smaller portions
* Eat food that is low in calories and high in nutrients
* Eat more fruits, vegetables and whole grains
* Eat less fats and fatty foods
* Eat less sugar and sweets
* Increase your physical activities and exercise regularly

**3. Avoid foods rich in fat, especially saturated fat and cholesterol**
* Use skimmed or low fat milk and milk products
* Decrease use of egg yolks and organ meats
* Choose fish, skinless chicken and lean meat
* Bake, broil, roast, steam or boil rather than frying

**4. Eat foods with adequate fibers**
* All fruits and vegetables that can be eaten with skin, should be eaten with skin, for instance carrot, cucumber, apple, chickoo etc.
* Use whole grains and their products like bran instead of refined flours like maida
* Eat sprouts and pulses
* Eat plenty of green leafy vegetables

**5. Avoid too much sugar**
* White sugar, jaggery, honey, syrups, soft drinks, candies, chocolates, cakes and cookies
* Avoid eating sweets between meals
* Select processed fruits without sugar syrups
* Select unsweetened fruit juices

**6. Avoid too much sodium**
* Learn to enjoy the flavours of unsalted foods
* Cook with only small amount of salt
* Try flavouring foods with herbs, spices, lemon juice, tomatoes, tamarind juice and curds
* Avoid adding salt to food at the table
* Avoid salty foods such as chips and other fried foods
* Limit the use of processed and preserved foods like pickles, sauces, cheese, *papads*, and alike which have a high sodium content as preservation

**7. Limit the intake of beverages**
* Alcoholic drinks – they are high in calories and low in nutrients. Overall the metabolites (end products) produced by alcohol are harmful especially to the liver in the body.

However a glass of red wine a day is being propagated these days. My personal feeling is that similar or better results can be achieved from other healthy sources.

* Soft drinks – they supply only 'empty calories' and no other nutrient. Diet soft drinks are low in calories but very high in sodium.

**8. Drink at least 8-10 glasses of water every day**

Water which is not generally classified as a nutrient, must not be overlooked. Lack of water even for a short period can be life threatening. An adult may consume 400 litres of water a year. About an equal amount is obtained from food. In a tropical country like India, it is imperative that at least 8-10 glasses of water are consumed every day to replace fluid loss.

**9. Physical activity and exercise**

Healthy and tasty eating without adequate and regular exercise is meaningless. To increase your activity, pick an exercise routine that suits your life style so that you will stick to it. Thirty minutes of aerobic exercise at least three to five times a week is a good idea. If you cannot join a gym or you are not interested in recreational sports like tennis, badminton, golf etc.; find other ways to be physically active. Some suggestions:

* Walk to and fro to work or walk a part of it
* Skip the elevator and walk up and down the stairs
* Leave your vehicle some distance from where you have headed so you can walk partly
* Go for morning or evening brisk walks with your partner or spouse. It always works better than going for a walk alone.

# ACKNOWLEDGEMENTS

Anil Bhandari
Anil Jain
Casabella, Morarjee Mills
Chef Inder Dev
Chef Ganesh
Chef Rajiv Julka
Chefs of India
Clea PR
Dr. Chetan Bhatt
Dr. Meena & Ram Prabhoo
Dr. Sujata Udeshi
Ergotech Studio, Pune
Ganesh Pednekar
Gokarn Enterprises
Jayakumar
Jijesh Gangadharan
Khazana Restaurant, Dubai
National School of Cooking
Nina Murdeshwar
Mr. & Mrs. Kalyanpur
Parag Agarwal
Pravin Gharat
Rahee Dahake
Rama B. Udeshi
Ranjit Kate
Sakshi Udeshi
Sanjiv & Namrata Bahl
Smeeta Bhatkal
Tanishq Consultants, New Delhi
ZEE Television

# CONTENTS

# SALADS

Salads are not new to the world of food, but their use has broadened. Salads not only complement a meal, but can be a dieter's salvation. Salads mean a lot of eating without loads of calories. Salads with sensible oil based dressings, are often very low in calories and yet packed with nutrition.

Salads can be served as appetizers or as a main course. A salad can be as simple as a colourful bowl of tossed greens or as complex as a main dish that may take hours to prepare. Salads are a symphony of tastes and textures where individual flavours are recognized but the combined effect is pleasant harmony.

**Nutritive value:** Salads, which are vegetable-based, are rich in vitamins like B complex, Vitamin C, B-carotene, folic acid. Minerals like calcium, iron, potassium are also present in good amount in vegetables, especially greens like lettuce, celery and broccoli. Salads are eaten raw or just tossed in some seasoning and hence give a lot of roughage or fiber. Fiber also plays an important role in avoiding constipation, lowering cholesterol and triglyceride, decreasing absorption of sugar, and fighting cancer. Beans or sprouts based salads are high in proteins. Sprouts have good amount of riboflavin and Vitamin C. When combined with pastas like macaroni, spaghetti or roots like potatoes or sweet potatoes they will also give carbohydrate.

Using red or organ meat as a main component or an accompaniment will give more fat and cholesterol. Chicken, fish are a good source of protein and are a better alternative to red organ meat.

Many health conscious people like to have a meal of soup and salad or soup and sandwich or soup, salad and a low calorie dessert. These too if chosen wisely, can form a complete meal, supplying various nutrients in the desired amount.

**Soups and Salads as a meal:** If one chooses a light soup, then the salad should be complimented in such a way that it will not only be filling but supply enough nutrients too. For instance

* Soup: Carrot soup to which no thickening or fat, butter, cream is added.
* Salad: Beans salad accompanied with wheat bread toast.

**Nutrition:** Carrots will supply B–carotene. Beans salad will supply protein, B complex, iron. Whole wheat bread used will supply carbohydrate, fiber and B complex. In general this meal will be low calorie, high in nutrients and fiber.

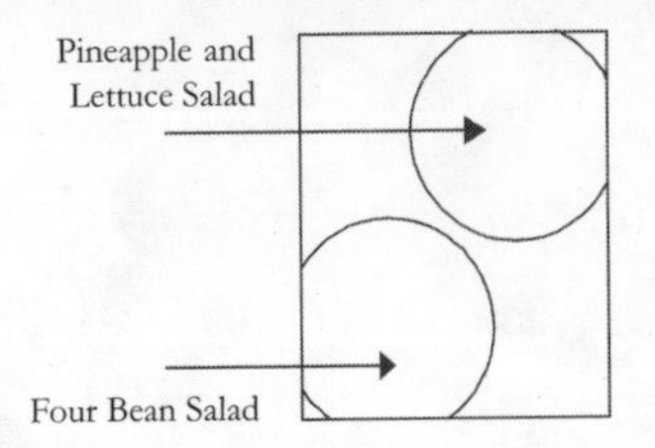


# FOUR BEAN
## *Salad*

### INGREDIENTS

White (Cow) beans (*Chowli*) ........... ¼ cup
Red kidney beans (*Rajma*) ............. ¼ cup
Green grams (Whole *Moong*) ......... ¼ cup
French beans ............................100 gms
Onion............................ 1 medium sized
Fresh coriander ................................ ½ cup
Mint....................................................... ¼ cup
Green chillies .......................................... 2
Lemon juice.................................. 3 tblspns
*Chaat Masala* ............................... 1 ½ tspn

### METHOD OF PREPARATION

1. Pick and wash white cow beans and kidney beans separately.
2. Soak them separately, overnight in plenty of water. Wash and soak the green *moong* beans for about two hours.
3. Boil the three dry beans separately in salted water till soft. Drain and let them cool.
4. String the french beans and cut into one-fourth inch pieces. Boil in salted boiling water till done. Drain immediately (you may reserve the cooking liquid to use as stock for some other recipe) and refresh with cold water. Drain and keep aside.
5. Peel and cut onion into one-fourth inch sized pieces. Clean, wash, drain and chop green coriander and mint. Wash and chop green chillies finely. Peel and wash and chop it.
6. Dilute lemon juice with equal amount of water. Stir in chopped green coriander, mint, green chillies and *chaat masala*. Shake well and refrigerate the dressing for at least an hour.
7. Mix all the cooked beans with diced onion and add the dressing. Toss the salad to evenly mix the dressing.

**Chef's Tip:**

*Do not hesitate to throw away the water in which you soak pulses as it is going to be more harmful than beneficial.*

### NUTRITIONAL INFORMATION

| Calories | Proteins | Fat | Carbohydrates | Fibre |
|---|---|---|---|---|
| 85 | 5.5 | 0.7 | 15 | 1.5 |

Soaking, draining and then cooking of pulses is important to destroy the anti-nutritional factors like tripsin-inhibitor, phytates etc.

Tripsin-inhibitor reduces protein digestibility. Soaking and heating the legumes help destroy the tripsin-inhibitor and improve protein quality.

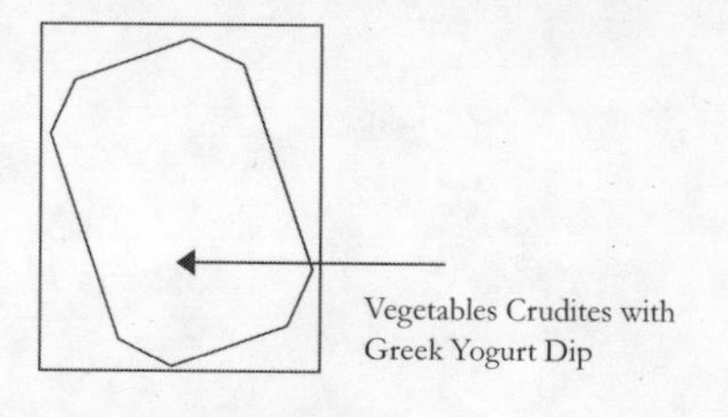
Vegetables Crudites with Greek Yogurt Dip

# VEGETABLE CRUDITES

## *with Greek Yogurt Dip*

### INGREDIENTS

Mint leaves ........................................ ¼ cup
Garlic ............................................ 4 cloves
Cherry tomatoes ................................. 8-10
Carrots ......................................... 2 medium
White radish .............................. 1 medium
Red radish ............................................ 4
Iceberg lettuce ......................... 8-10 leaves
Cucumbers ................................ 2 medium
Skimmed milk yogurt ..................... 4 cups
Sesame seeds (white) .................... ¼ tspn
Lemon juice ........................................ 1 tspn
Salt ............................................... to taste

### METHOD OF PREPARATION

1. Clean mint leaves, wash and reserve some for decoration and chop the remaining. Peel and chop garlic finely.
2. Wash the cherry tomatoes and cut them into halves.
3. Peel carrots, wash and cut into finger sized pieces. Peel white radish, wash and cut into finger sized pieces.
4. Wash red radish and quarter each. Waşh lettuce leaves and soak in chilled water. Peel cucumber, wash and cut into finger sized pieces.
5. Hang skimmed milk yogurt in a muslin cloth to remove excess water. Toast the sesame seeds lightly and cool.
6. Combine thick yogurt with chopped mint, lemon juice, white sesame seeds and garlic. Mix thoroughly. Add salt to taste and chill.
7. Just before serving drain the lettuce leaves and spread on a serving plate, arrange the prepared vegetables decoratively and serve with the chilled dressing.

### NUTRITIONAL INFORMATION

| Calories | Proteins | Fat | Carbohydrates | Fibre |
|---|---|---|---|---|
| 65 | 3.2 | 0.8 | 12.5 | 1.2 |

Today, a variety of dips like sauces, ketchup, and chutneys are readily available in the market. Most of them have a high concentration of preservatives and added colour. Both preservatives and colour are known to have their ill-effects on health. So, as far as possible do go in for home-made dips and chutneys, which will be both safe and nutritious.

# JELLIED TOMATO

## *Pots*

### INGREDIENTS

Tomatoes ...................... 6 medium sized
Garlic ............................................ 2 cloves
Gelatin powder ............................... 10 gms
Bay leaves ........................................... 2
Crushed pepper corn ..................... ½ tspn
Mixed herbs ................................... ½ tspn
Salt .............................................. to taste
Port wine (optional) ............... 4 tblspns
Skimmed milk yogurt ..................... ¼ cup
Lemon juice .................................. 2 tspns
Fresh mint...................................... 4 sprigs

### METHOD OF PREPARATION

1. Wash and finely chop the tomatoes. Peel garlic and crush. Soak the gelatin in quarter cup cold water and keep.
2. Cook the tomatoes in a saucepan along with the crushed garlic, bay leaves and crushed pepper corn for about five to six minutes or until soft.
3. Remove from the heat, cover and leave to infuse for twenty minutes.
4. Remove the bay leaves, puree the mixture and pass through a sieve.
5. Stir in the mixed herbs, salt and wine. Whisk the Skimmed milk yogurt and mix into the tomato mixture.
6. Heat the gelatin lightly on a double boiler to dissolve and add to the tomato mixture. Mix in the lemon juice and stir well.
7. Pour this into small ceramic pots for individual serving. Refrigerate for three to four hours to set. Do not freeze.
8. Serve chilled in the same pot garnished with sprigs of fresh mint.

### NUTRITIONAL INFORMATION

| Calories | Proteins | Fat | Carbohydrates | Fibre |
|---|---|---|---|---|
| 40 | 2. 0 | 0.2 | 5. 8 | 0. 7 |

Wines are available in countless varieties. Research claims health benefits, but like anything else overdose can harm the body. There are claims that wine helps fight cancer, heals ulcers and lowers cholesterol.

Sulfites are higher in white wine than in red. Some people are sensitive to the natural sulfites found in wine. Others get migraine headaches from too many tannins which are mostly found in red wine.

Calorie chart:
Sweet wine — 160 calories per glass
Unsweetened wine — 50 calories per glass

# HEALTHY SALAD

## *in Garlic Dressing*

**INGREDIENTS**

Eggs .................... 4
Spinach .................... 16-20 leaves
Lettuce .................... 16-20 leaves
Red pepper .................... 1 medium sized
Tomatoes .................... 4 medium sized
Pineapple .................... 4 slices
Baby corns .................... 6-8
Garlic .................... 8-10 cloves
Malt vinegar .................... 2 tblspns
Virgin olive oil .................... 1 tblspn
Mustard paste .................... 1 tblspn
Salt .................... to taste
Black pepper powder .................... ¼ tspn
Brown sugar .................... 1 tspn

**METHOD OF PREPARATION**

1. Cook eggs in boiling water for about ten to twelve minutes. Remove and cool them in water.
2. Peel, halve and remove the yolks. Use only whites. You may reserve the yolks for some other purpose. Cut the boiled egg whites into thick strips.
3. Wash the spinach and lettuce leaves in running water thoroughly. Drain and tear them roughly.
4. Wash and wipe red pepper dry. Apply very little oil on the red pepper and roast in a very hot oven till blisters form on the pepper. Alternately you can roast red pepper on an open flame also. Cool a little and peel the top skin. Halve the pepper, deseed and cut into one and a half inch long strips.
5. Wash and cut tomatoes into halves and deseed. Cut them into one and a half inch long strip. Cut pineapple slices into one and a half inch long strips.
6. If the baby corns are tender, cut them lengthwise into strips and use raw. Otherwise blanch them in salted water for five to seven minutes, cool and use.
7. Peel and chop garlic. Combine malt vinegar, virgin olive oil, garlic, mustard paste, salt, brown sugar and black pepper powder.
8. Mix egg white strips, red pepper, baby corn, tomatoes and pineapple. Gently mix with lettuce and spinach leaves. Add the prepared dressing on to the salad and toss it. Serve cold.

**NUTRITIONAL INFORMATION**

| Calories | Proteins | Fat | Carbohydrates | Fibre |
|---|---|---|---|---|
| 65 | 4.8 | 1.5 | 8 | 1 |

The protein quality of egg is of a very high quality. The quality of dietary protein depends on the pattern of essential amino acids it supplies. Egg proteins and human milk protein fulfill these criteria and are classified as high quality proteins. One egg yields 80 calories of which only sixteen are in white. Cholesterol and vitamin A, $B_{12}$, D and iron are all contained in the yolk. Raw egg white contains anti-nutritional factors, which are destroyed on cooking.

# LEAFY GREENS WITH APPLE

*and Caraway Vinaigrette*

### INGREDIENTS

Cabbage ................................ ¼ small sized
Iceberg lettuce ................ 1 medium sized
Leaf lettuce
(preferably Romaine) .................... 1 bunch
Tender spinach leaves ........... 16-20 leaves
Tender radish leaves .......................... 8-10
Dill leaves ........................................ ½ cup

**Dressing**

Caraway seeds .............................. 1 tspn
Apple juice ...................... ½ cup (120 ml.)
Olive oil ........................................ 1 tblspn
Red wine vinegar ......................... 4 tblspn
Paprika or red chilli powder ......... ¼ tspn
Honey .................................................. 1 tspn
Black pepper (crushed) ................. ½ tspn
Salt ............................................... to taste

### METHOD OF PREPARATION

**Chef's Tip:** *If Red wine vinegar is not easily available, use malt vinegar instead.*

1. Roast the caraway seeds on a dry *tawa*, cool and crush well.
2. Mix all the dressing ingredients in a bottle, close tightly and shake well. Refrigerate till you require.
3. Wash cabbage and cut into one inch sized pieces.
4. Clean and wash iceberg lettuce, leaf lettuce, tender spinach, tender radish, dill leaves in lots of water, then trim and refresh in chilled water.
5. Tear the leaves into bite size pieces, mix well and refrigerate to keep them crisp.
6. Just before serving, pour the prepared dressing and toss. Serve cold.

### NUTRITIONAL INFORMATION

| Calories | Proteins | Fat | Carbohydrates | Fibre |
|---|---|---|---|---|
| 80 | 1.4 | 4.2 | 12 | 0. 8 |

Dill Leaves is a leafy vegetable commonly known as *Soowa* or *Shepu.* It is rich in B-carotene, iron, calcium, and Vitamin B complex. It is advisable to first wash all leafy vegetable under running water and then cut, to prevent loss of water-soluble nutrients.

Dill leaves are known to aid digestion. They also promote the flow of breast milk in lactating mothers.

# KOREAN PICKLED
## *Vegetables*

### INGREDIENTS

Red radish (round) ........... 3-4 small sized
White radish .............................. 1 medium
Fresh mushrooms ....................... 200 gms
Carrots ...................................... 2 medium
Cauliflower ..................... ½ medium sized
Garlic ................................................ 6-8
Green chillies ..................................... 3-4
Spring onions ........................................ 3
Ginger ...................................... 1 inch knob
Soya sauce ..................................... 1 tblspns
Black pepper ........................................ 1 tspn
Dried red chillies ........................................ 2
Lemon leaves ........................................ 2-3
Star anise .............................................. 1-2
Salt ................................................ to taste
White vinegar ..................................... ¾ cup

### METHOD OF PREPARATION

1. Wash, trim and quarter the red radish. Peel, wash and cut white radish into one and a half inch long thin strips. Wash mushrooms with plenty of water and then cut into quarters. Peel and wash carrots, and cut into one and a half inch long thin strips.
2. Cut the cauliflower into small florets, wash and soak in warm salted water for ten to fifteen minutes. Drain and keep aside.
3. Peel the garlic and wash the green chillies and keep them whole. Peel, wash and trim the spring onion, discard the green leaves and reserve the onion whole.
4. Scrape the ginger, wash well and cut into thin slices.
5. Heat two and a half cups water with soya sauce, sliced ginger, black pepper, Dried red chillies, lemon leaves, peeled garlic, star anise and salt to taste. Bring to boil, reduce flame and simmer for two to three minutes.
6. Add the white vinegar and the prepared vegetables including the green chillies. Remove from heat immediately and stir well.
7. Pour into a glass or ceramic jar and cool. Cover the jar with a muslin cloth and let the vegetables pickle for two days at room temperature, before using. Stir two to three times a day for uniform pickling.
8. Refrigerate and use a slotted spoon to remove the pickle as and when required. It has a shelf life of two to three weeks.

### NUTRITIONAL INFORMATION

| Calories | Proteins | Fat | Carbohydrates | Fibre |
|---|---|---|---|---|
| 70 | 3.14 | 0.7 | 13 | 1.8 |

Pickles are very commonly eaten in India. Salt, sugar and oil are mainly used as preservatives, but they can do more harm than good. Salt is a concentrated source of sodium whereas sugar and oil give plenty of calories. However, if one would like to consume pickles, a better alternative is the use of vinegar or lemon juice as preservatives. Further, refrigeration can help to increase the shelf life of pickled vegetables with minimum amount of preservatives used.

# PEPPERY CORNS AND
## *Tomato Salad*

### INGREDIENTS

Whole corn kernels ........................ 2 cups
Yellow capsicum (optional) .... 1 medium sized
Green capsicum .............. 2 medium sized
Pineapple ....................................... 4 slices
Tomatoes .......................... 3 medium sized
Green chillies ........................................ 1-2
Mint leaves ........................................ ½ cup
Pepper corns .................................... 15-20
Lemon juice ................................ 2 tblspns
Salt ..................................................... to taste

### METHOD OF PREPARATION

1. Boil corn kernels in salted water until soft. Drain thoroughly and cool. You may also use precooked canned corn kernels or sweet corn niblets. Wash them thoroughly before use.
2. Wash, halve, deseed yellow capsicum and green capsicum and then dice into one cm. sized pieces. Similarly cut pineapple slices into one cm. sized pieces.
3. Wash tomatoes, cut into quarters, deseed and then dice into one cm. sized pieces.
4. Wash green chillies, remove stem and then chop them. Clean, wash and chop mint leaves. Crush pepper corns.
5. Combine corn kernels, yellow pepper, green pepper, tomatoes and pineapple. Stir in lemon juice and add crushed pepper corns, salt, chopped green chillies and chopped mint leaves.
6. Arrange in a serving dish and chill before serving.

### NUTRITIONAL INFORMATION

| Calories | Proteins | Fat | Carbohydrates | Fibre |
|---|---|---|---|---|
| 60 | 2.2 | 0.4 | 13.5 | 1.1 |

Tomatoes have a good amount of Vitamin C (in uncooked form) and B-carotene. While making homemade puree, sauces and soups, do not discard the skin, as it is the source of fibre. Flavonoids that are present in ripe tomatoes are known to provide protection from certain types of cancer.

# MINTED
## *Mushrooms*

**INGREDIENTS**

| | | | |
|---|---|---|---|
| Mushrooms | 400 gms | Mint leaves | 1 cup |
| Lemon juice | 2 tblspns | Skimmed milk yogurt | 3 tblspns |
| Tomato | 1 medium sized | Salt | to taste |
| Cucumber | 1 medium sized | Cabbage or lettuce leaves | 4 to 5 |

**METHOD OF PREPARATION**

1. Clean and wash mushrooms and then cut into quarters.
2. Put mushrooms in a thick-bottomed vessel along with lemon juice and a little salt. Stew them over low heat for ten minutes. Keep aside.
3. Wash, halve, deseed tomato and dice into one cm. sized pieces. Peel cucumber and dice it into one cm sized pieces.
4. Clean, wash mint leaves, reserve one or two sprigs for garnishing and chop the rest.
5. Combine mushrooms with diced tomato, diced cucumber and chopped mint. Mix in Skimmed milk yogurt and salt and toss lightly.
6. Serve on a bed of cabbage leaves or lettuce leaves garnished with a sprig of mint leaves.

**NUTRITIONAL INFORMATION**

| Calories | Proteins | Fat | Carbohydrates | Fibre |
|---|---|---|---|---|
| 60 | 4.0 | 1.0 | 8 | 0.7 |

Mint is a good source of B-carotene, iron, calcium, B complex and Vitamin C. Usually mint is eaten uncooked in the form of dressing or *chutney*. There is a good amount of Vitamin C and B complex in green leafy vegetables, but they are destroyed on cooking. Hence it is a good practice to eat mint, green coriander and others in the uncooked form. Mint is also known to aid digestion.

# GULMARG

*Salad*

## INGREDIENTS

Apples ............................ 2 medium sized
Lemon juice ............................ 2 tblspns
Tomatoes ........................ 2 medium sized
Carrot ............................ 1 medium sized
Orange ............................................ 1
Coriander leaves ............................ ¼ cup
Mint leaves ...................................... ¼ cup
Spring onions ................ 2 medium sized
Fresh button mushrooms ............... 8-10
Lettuce ................................................ 8
Dried red chillies ................................. 2
Salad oil ........................................ 1 tblspn
Salt ............................................... to taste
Bean sprouts .................................. ¾ cup

## METHOD OF PREPARATION

1. Core and cut apples into quarters with the skin and thinly slice and sprinkle a little lemon juice and mix lightly. Wash tomatoes and cut into quarters and slice.
2. Wash, peel and cut carrots lengthwise and slice them thin. Peel the orange and discard the seeds and pith. Cut the segments into two.
3. Clean, wash and chop coriander and mint leaves. Wash, trim and slice the spring onion with the greens.
4. Wash the mushrooms thoroughly, drain and slice them. Mix with some lemon juice to prevent discolouring.
5. Trim the lettuce leaves, wash in flowing water and soak in chilled water, to keep them fresh and crisp. Trim, deseed and shred the dried red chillies into flakes.
6. Mix the remaining lemon juice, salad oil, red chilli flakes, chopped coriander and mint leaves. Add salt to taste. Whisk well.
7. Drain the lettuce leaves and tear them into bite-sized pieces. Make a bed of these leaves on the serving dish. Lace with one fourth part of the dressing.
8. Combine sliced apples, bean sprouts, orange segments, sliced carrots, sliced mushrooms, sliced tomatoes and sliced spring onion.
9. Toss them in the remaining dressing and place it on the lettuce bed. Serve immediately.

## NUTRITIONAL INFORMATION

| Calories | Proteins | Fat | Carbohydrates | Fibre |
|---|---|---|---|---|
| 135 | 3.1 | 5.5 | 20.7 | 2.2 |

One apple will give around 60-80 cals. and a fair amount of choline. Apples are rich in soluble fibre, called pectin which reduces cholesterol and regulates blood sugar. One medium size apple with peel can provide 3.5 gms. fibre and without the peel, the fibre content is 2.7gms. For its fibre content, apple is best eaten with the peel, but apples, like several fruits are not only treated with insecticides, but also sprayed with a coating of wax to prevent moisture losses. So it is advisable to wash and scrub applés under running water before they are eaten.

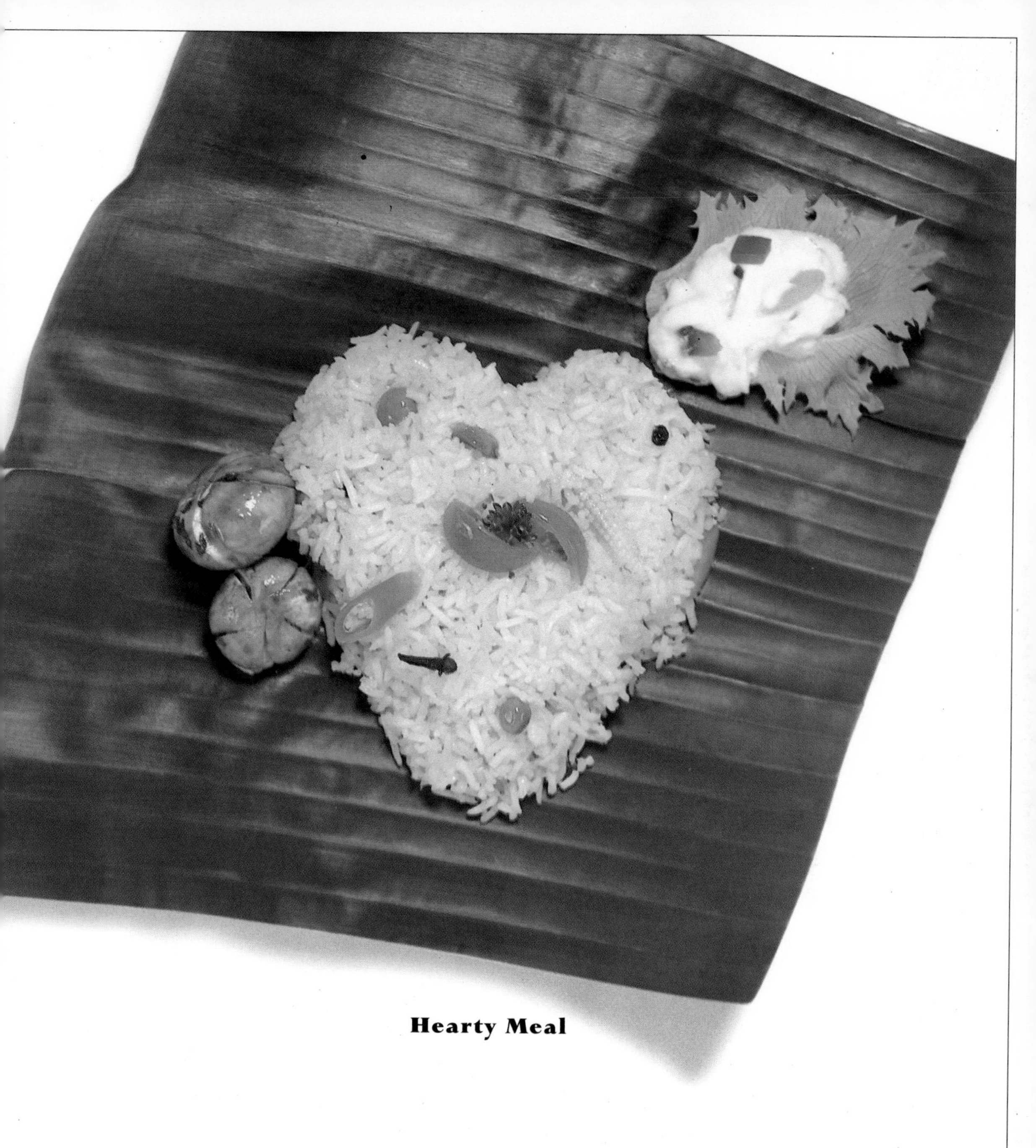

Hearty Meal

Delicious and nutritious food you can eat to your heart's content.

# CRUNCHY VEGETABLE
## *Salad*

### INGREDIENTS

Red cabbage ........................ ½ small
Green cabbage ........................ ½ small
Carrots ........................ 2 medium sized
White radish ........................ 2 medium sized
Capsicum ........................ 2 medium sized
Bean sprouts ........................ 2 cups
Roasted peanuts ........................ ½ cup
Oil ........................ 2 tspn
Orange juice ........................ 5 tblspns
Mustard paste ........................ 1 tspn
Lemon juice ........................ 1 tblspn
Salt ........................ to taste
White pepper powder ........................ to taste

### METHOD OF PREPARATION

1. Shred the red cabbage and green cabbage.
2. Peel, wash and grate carrots and white radish.
3. Wash, halve and deseed capsicums and then chop.
4. Wash bean sprouts and drain completely.
5. Crush roasted peanuts coarsely.
6. Mix oil, orange juice, mustard paste, lemon juice, salt and white pepper powder thoroughly. Keep aside in the refrigerator.
7. In a serving bowl arrange red cabbage at the bottom then layer with green cabbage, carrots, radish, capsicum and then bean sprouts. Chill in a refrigerator.
8. Put roasted crushed peanuts on top.
9. Shake the dressing thoroughly and lace the salad with the dressing uniformly just before serving.

### NUTRITIONAL INFORMATION

| Calories | Proteins | Fat | Carbohydrates | Fibre |
|---|---|---|---|---|
| 145 | 6.7 | 6 | 17 | 2 |

Carrot is an important source of B-carotene, choline and fibre (especially in raw form). It is also known to purify the blood and tonify the kidney. B-carotene that is converted to Vitamin A in the body, plays important role in good vision, bone development, skin integrity, immunity, reproduction, and anti-cancer functions.

# ROASTED POTATO

## *Salad*

### INGREDIENTS

Potatoes .......................... 8 medium sized
Cumin seeds .............................. ½ tspn
Dried pomegranate
seeds (*Anardana*) .............................. 1 tspn
Fresh coriander leaves .................... ¼ cup
Spring onion ................. 1 medium sized
Ground black Salt ......................... to taste
Black pepper powder ..................... ½ tspn
Red chilli powder .......................... ¼ tspn
Tamarind pulp ................................ 1 tspn

### METHOD OF PREPARATION

1. Wash potatoes, dry and then prick them with a fork.
2. Spread one cm. thick layer of salt on a roasting/baking tray. Place potatoes without touching each other on the tray.
3. Cook in a preheated oven at 200 degrees Celsius for twenty five to thirty minutes or till cooked. Alternately cook in a microwave oven for seven to eight minutes on HIGH. Cool them completely.
4. Cut roasted potatoes along with their skin into one inch sized pieces.
5. Roast cumin seeds on a hot *tawa* for half a minute, stirring continuously. Remove and add pomegranate seeds (*anardana*) and grind to powder.
6. Clean, wash and chop fresh coriander leaves. Peel, wash and chop spring onion.
7. Mix roasted cumin seed powder, ground black salt, black pepper powder, red chilli powder, fresh coriander leaves and spring onion. Add tamarind pulp and mix thoroughly. Add a little water if required.
8. Toss the roasted potato pieces in this dressing.
9. Arrange in a serving dish and serve.

**Chef's Tip:**

*Adding one to two potatoes to any other vegetable can help improve the taste and flavour. It can also increase the consumption of other vegetables.*

### NUTRITIONAL INFORMATION

| Calories | Proteins | Fat | Carbohydrates | Fibre |
|---|---|---|---|---|
| 75 | 1.3 | 0.2 | 18 | 0.6 |

Potatoes eaten in small quantities and in the right form can be nourishing and tasteful. Compared to other vegetables potato has higher calories— 100 cals/100 gms. Potatoes are a good source of potassium, thiamin (B1), niacin, folic acid and choline. It is advisable to cook potatoes with skin as the skin has more nutrients; however scrub them thoroughly before cooking. Also discard the sprouts and green spots as they contain the toxin called solanin which, when consumed in high amounts, can cause headaches, irritation of the throat etc. While steaming, roasting and cooking, do not cut potatoes, to avoid leaching of nutrients, especially water soluble nutrients like potassium, niacin etc.

Deep fried potato chips are considered junk food, due to the high proportion of salt and oil in them.

# PINEAPPLE AND LETTUCE

## *Salad*

### INGREDIENTS

Pineapple .................................... 6 slices
Iceberg lettuce ........................ 16-20 leaves
Cucumber .................................. 2 medium
Lemon juice ................................ 2 tblspns
Pineapple juice ........................... 3 tblspns
Honey ............................................. 1 tblspn
Salt ............................................... to taste
Dried mixed herbs ......................... ¼ tspn
Crushed pepper corns ..................... 1 tspn
White pepper powder ...................... ¼ tspn

### METHOD OF PREPARATION

1. Cut pineapple into three fourth inch sized pieces.
2. Wash and keep iceberg lettuce in ice cold water for about fifteen minutes.
3. Peel cucumber, wash and cut into half lengthwise and remove seeds. Then cut cucumber into three fourth inch sized pieces.
4. Mix lemon juice, pineapple juice, honey, salt, mixed herbs, crushed pepper corns and white pepper powder. Leave aside for at least fifteen minutes.
5. Tear lettuce leaves into bite-sized pieces and combine with pineapple and cucumber pieces.
6. Pour the dressing on the salad and toss lightly. Serve immediately.

**Chef's Tip:**

*Fresh herbs can either be sundried or can be dried in a warm oven. Store in an air tight container or bottle for future use.*

### NUTRITIONAL INFORMATION

| Calories | Proteins | Fat | Carbohydrates | Fibre |
|---|---|---|---|---|
| 40 | 0.7 | 0.5 | 4 | 0. 7 |

One slice of fresh pineapple will contain about 20 to 30 calories. Pineapple is also rich in Vitamin C and complex carbohydrates (fibre). Canned pineapple has very little Vitamin C as it is destroyed on cooking. Sugar syrup in the can adds to unnecessary "empty" calories and preservatives may give high amount of sodium.

# GOLDEN CHICKEN

## *Salad*

**Chef's Tip:**

*As a variation to this salad you may tear the leaves of the lettuce and mix into the salad.*

### INGREDIENTS

Chicken breasts, boneless ...... 4 medium sized
Apples, golden ................ 4 medium sized
Lemon juice .................................. 2 tspns
Pineapple ....................................... 2 slices
Lettuce .................................... 8-10 leaves
Celery ...................... 1 medium sized stalk
Walnut kernels ................................... 8-10
Skimmed milk yogurt ...................... 1 cup
Salt ................................................ to taste
White pepper powder .................... to taste

### METHOD OF PREPARATION

1. Cut chicken breasts into bite-sized (approx. half inch) pieces. Poach in salted water, drain and then cool thoroughly.
2. Core apples and cut with the skin into half inch sized pieces. Add lemon juice and mix well.
3. Cut pineapple slices into half inch sized pieces.
4. Wash lettuce leaves in running water and soak in chilled water. Wash and chop celery stalk. Soak walnuts in hot water for a few minutes. Reserve a few walnut kernels whole for garnishing and chop the rest.
5. Hang the skimmed milk yogurt in a muslin cloth for about fifteen minutes to remove excess liquid.
6. Mix chicken, apples, pineapple, chopped walnuts and celery. Add the hung yogurt. Add salt and white pepper powder to taste.
7. Spread lettuce leaves on a serving dish and arrange the salad on them.
8. Garnish with walnut kernels.

### NUTRITIONAL INFORMATION

| Calories | Proteins | Fat | Carbohydrates | Fibre |
|---|---|---|---|---|
| 180 | 11.3 | 9.6 | 13 | 1 |

One of the important nutrients lemon has is Vitamin C or ascorbic acid. Vitamin C is essential for normal functions of all cells, promotes healing of wounds, fractures, bleeding gums, facilitates iron absorption from the intestine, helps the body to maintain resistance to infection and above all has antioxidant properties.

# SPICY PINEAPPLE
## *Boat*

**INGREDIENTS**

Pineapple ........................ 1 medium sized
Apples ............................ 2 medium sized
Papaya ................................ 1 small sized
Green chillies ................................. 2-3
Pears .............................. 2 medium sized
Pomegranate ............................ ½ medium
Oranges ......................... 2 medium sized
Lemon juice ................................. 1 tblspn
Ground black salt ..................... to taste
Orange juice ............................ 3 tblspns

**METHOD OF PREPARATION**

1. Halve the pineapple lengthwise. Scoop the flesh out without damaging the shell and cut the flesh into one cm. sized pieces.
2. Wash, core and cut apples into one cm. cubes.
3. Peel, halve, deseed and cut papaya into one cm. cubes.
4. Wash green chillies and grind to a coarse paste.
5. Wash and cut pears into one cm. cubes. Separate pomegranate pearls from the pomegranate.
6. Peel orange, remove segments, discard seeds and cut each orange segment into three pieces.
7. Mix all fruits with lemon juice, green chilli paste, ground black salt and orange juice. Serve this in the halved pineapple boats.

*Chef's Tip:*

*Since this dish is rich in minerals like potassium, it can prevent muscle cramps.*

**NUTRITIONAL INFORMATION**

| Calories | Proteins | Fat | Carbohydrates | Fibre |
|---|---|---|---|---|
| 135 | 1.5 | 0.7 | 31.8 | 2.5 |

Ripe papaya has a good amount of Vitamin C and B-carotene. The carotene gets converted to vitamin A in our body. Both vitamin C and B carotene have anti-oxidant property. However, seeds of papaya should not be eaten along with the fruit as they contain a toxic substance called carpine in them. Papain enzyme present in papaya helps digestion.

There are many kinds of soups that suit different occasions, at various times. Thin, clear or light soups can be used as a starter to a meal. Filling, creamy soups can almost be a complete meal in themselves. Hot and spicy soups taste great on a cold and rainy day whereas chilled soups serve as a perfect start to a summer meal.

The essentials of a well-made soup would be its pleasing and natural colour and a mild flavour that is not over powering. The soup should be non-greasy. The consistency of cream soups should be that of fresh cream and that of clear soups should be a little thicker than water. The seasoning should be sufficient but not in excess.

The nutritive value of soups varies, depending upon the exact ingredients used. Thin soups in general are lower in nutritive content as compared to thick soups. Chicken sweet corn and green pea soups are especially valuable for their protein content. A bowl of spinach soup provides one third of an adult's daily iron requirement. Cream soups approximately supply, on an average 275 calories, 10 gms. protein and 200 mg. of calcium per 250 mls. serving.

From the nutritional viewpoint, soups can be classified as —

Protein rich soup: Chicken, fish, egg, meat, lentils and beans are the main ingredients.

Vitamin and mineral rich soup: Vegetables like spinach, celery, carrot, peas, sprouts, cabbage, and lettuce and alike are used as a base.

South Indian preparations like *rasam* and *saaru*, Maharashtrian *saar* and *Osaman* from Gujarat fall under the category of light soups. They have different types of vegetables as a base, are a good source of Vitamins and minerals, and are low in calories.

# BEANS AND VEGETABLE

*Soup*

## INGREDIENTS

Red kidney beans (*Rajma*) .......... 1/3 cup
Onion .......... 1 medium sized
Garlic .......... 4 cloves
Carrot .......... 1 medium sized
Button mushrooms .......... ½ cup
French beans .......... 10-15
Tomatoes .......... 2 medium sized
Capsicum .......... 1 medium sized
Cucumber .......... 1 medium sized
Fresh coriander leaves .......... for garnish
Vegetable stock or water .......... 3 cups
Salt .......... to taste
Red chilli powder .......... ½ tspn.

## METHOD OF PREPARATION

1. Soak red kidney beans in sufficient water overnight. Pressure cook along with peeled and chopped onion and garlic. Cook until kidney beans are soft, drain and reserve the cooking liquor. Mash kidney beans lightly and keep aside.
2. Peel, wash and cut carrot into small dices (half cm. sized). Clean, wash and cut mushrooms in small pieces. String french beans, wash them and cut into small dices.
3. Wash tomatoes and puree them in a blender. Wash capsicum, cut it into half and remove seeds and cut into half cm. sized dices. Peel cucumber, remove seeds and cut into half cm. sized dices. Clean and wash fresh coriander leaves. Separate leaves from the stems, discard stems and reserve coriander leaves for garnishing.
4. Mix lightly mashed kidney beans with the cooking liquor. Stir in pureed tomatoes and bring it to a boil.
5. Add carrots, french beans and vegetable stock or water. Continue to simmer till carrots are cooked. Stir in diced mushrooms, salt, red chilli powder and diced capsicum. Simmer for five minutes and add diced cucumber.
6. Serve hot garnished with fresh coriander leaves.

## NUTRITIONAL INFORMATION

| Calories | Proteins | Fat | Carbohydrates | Fibre |
|---|---|---|---|---|
| 55 | 2.3 | 1.3 | 10 | 1.3 |

Red kidney beans (*Rajma*) have about 23-25% proteins and 5% fibre. *Rajma* is good source of many minerals like calcium, iron, magnesium, manganese, copper, zinc and chromium. Chromium is an important trace element required for normal glucose metabolism and related to normal function of insulin. Another good source of Chromium is Brewers Yeast.

# BROCCOLI AND TOASTED
## *Almond Soup*

### INGREDIENTS

Broccoli ........................................ 400 gms
Onion ............................ 1 medium sized
Garlic ............................................ 4 cloves
Celery stalk .................................. 2 inches
Almonds ............................................ 10-12
Stock or water ................................ 4 cups
Low fat milk ....................................... 1 cup
Salt .................................................. to taste
White pepper powder .................... to taste

### METHOD OF PREPARATION

1. Cut broccoli into small florets and wash well. Soak in salted water for ten to fifteen minutes and drain.
2. Peel and roughly chop onion and garlic. Wash and chop celery stalk.
3. Broil or dry roast almonds on medium heat till almond skin changes its colour slightly. Remove from heat, cool it and slice them into slivers.
4. Heat vegetable stock or water with chopped onion, garlic and celery. Bring it to a boil.
5. Add broccoli florets and continue to cook without covering the pan. Cook for five to seven minutes or till broccoli is tender.
6. Remove from fire, cool and puree it in a blender.
7. Add milk to pureed broccoli. Mix well. Bring to a boil again.
8. Add salt and white pepper powder to taste. Stir in tøasted almond slivers and serve hot.

### NUTRITIONAL INFORMATION

| Calories | Proteins | Fat | Carbohydrates | Fibre |
|---|---|---|---|---|
| 130 | 7.2 | 4.3 | 9.5 | 0.3 |

Broccoli looks like cauliflower but is dark green in colour. Broccoli being greener rates higher in nutritive value than cauliflower and is a good source of iron, phosphorous, vitamin A, ascorbic acid and riboflavin. The outer leaves of broccoli and cauliflower are much higher in nutritive value than the vegetables and should be used for cooking and salads. Broccoli has fibre and flavoids which help in fighting cancer.

**Health Food**

Tasty food is now good for your health.

us at www.saffola-india.com

**Fitness Buff's Delight**

Now maintain a healthy diet without compromising on taste.

Visit us at www.saffola-india.com

# MEDITERRANEAN SEAFOOD

*Soup*

## INGREDIENTS

| | | | |
|---|---|---|---|
| Seawater fish fillet | 150 gms | Bay leaves | 2 |
| River water fish fillet | 150 gms | Lemon rind | 1 tspn |
| Prawns | 8 medium sized | Dried red chilli | 1 |
| Baby Squids | 2 | Lemon juice | ½ tblspn |
| Parsley | 2-3 sprigs | Olive oil | 1 tblspn |
| Spinach | 8-10 leaves | Saffron | a pinch |
| Garlic | 2-3 cloves | Salt | to taste |

## METHOD OF PREPARATION

1. Clean, wash and cut fish fillet into one inch pieces.
2. Shell, devein and wash prawns thoroughly. Reserve the head and shell to make stock.
3. Clean and wash baby squids and cut each into six to eight rings.
4. Wash and chop parsley. Clean, wash and shred spinach leaves.
5. Heat one litre water with prawn heads, prawn shells, garlic, bay leaves and lemon rind. Break the red chilli into two and add. Simmer for fifteen to twenty minutes and remove from heat and rest the stock for ten minutes for the flavour and aroma to develop. Strain and keep warm.
6. Heat the olive oil in a saucepan, add the peeled prawn and squid rings. Sauté for a couple of minutes and add the fish pieces and stir gently.
7. Sprinkle the saffron and add the reserved stock and bring to a boil. Add salt, reduce the flame.
8. Add the shredded spinach and simmer till the seafood is soft and tender.
9. Sprinkle the chopped parsley, stir in the lemon juice and serve hot.

### NUTRITIONAL INFORMATION

| Calories | Proteins | Fat | Carbohydrates | Fibre |
|---|---|---|---|---|
| 75 | 9.9 | 1.6 | 2.1 | 0.1 |

Seawater fish is rich in Iodine and Flourine. Adequate intake of Flourine ensures strong and stable bones reducing incidence of osteoporosis, a condition where bones become fragile and porous, especially in old age. River water fish like Hilsa have high fat content as compared to seawater fish. One need not worry about this fat as most of it is unsaturated. Fish in general have unsaturated fatty acids, predominantly, omega-3, which have unique serum triglyceride lowering properties.

# MIXED VEGETABLE
## *Soup*

**INGREDIENTS**

Onion ............................ 1 medium sized
Carrot ............................ 1 medium sized
Potato ............................ 1 medium sized
Green cabbage ............... ¼ medium sized
French beans ............................ 6-8
Fresh mushrooms ............................ 6-8
Capsicum ............................ 1 medium sized
Cauliflower florets ............ 4-5 small sized
Oil ............................ 1 tblspn
Bay leaves ............................ 2
Whole meal flour ............................ 2 tspns
Salt ............................ to taste
White pepper powder ............................ to taste
Vegetable stock or water ............................ 2 cups
Skimmed milk ............................ 2 cups

**METHOD OF PREPARATION**

1. Peel onion, carrot and potato. Chop them as fine as possible. Keep the chopped potatoes soaked in water to avoid discolouration. Clean, trim and finely chop the cabbage.
2. String french beans and chop them real fine. Wash mushrooms, drain well and chop them fine. Wash, halve, deseed and finely chop the capsicum.
3. Wash and grate cauliflower florets along with the tender part of the stem.
4. Heat oil in a thick-bottomed saucepan, add the bay leaves and chopped onion and sauté for two minutes over medium heat. Drain the chopped potatoes and add.
5. Add the chopped carrots, chopped mushroom, chopped cabbage, chopped french beans and grated cauliflower. Stir and cook on high heat for three to four minutes.
6. Sprinkle the whole meal flour and cook for two minutes, stirring continuously over medium heat or till flour starts giving a cooked aroma. Add salt and white pepper powder.
7. Stir in the vegetable stock and bring to boil. Add the chopped capsicum. Reduce heat and simmer till the vegetables are cooked and the soup reaches a fairly thick consistency.
8. Gradually stir in the skimmed milk and simmer for three to four minutes.
9. Remove the bay leaf, adjust the seasoning and serve piping hot.

**NUTRITIONAL INFORMATION**

| Calories | Proteins | Fat | Carbohydrates | Fibre |
|---|---|---|---|---|
| 120 | 4.7 | 4.3 | 18.5 | 1.0 |

Vegetable stock is the liquid left behind when water, vegetables and flavourings have been simmered. Unlike meat stocks, vegetable stock needs special care while preparing. The vegetables used need to be thoroughly washed to get rid of any pesticides or dirt.

Cabbage, carrot, leeks, celery, onion and beans give their distinct flavour. Vegetable stock is a rich source of water soluble nutrients.

# CELESTIAL VEGETABLE
## *Soup*

**INGREDIENTS**

Button mushrooms ........................... 8-10
Carrot ............................ 1 medium sized
Capsicum ........................ 1 medium sized
Shelled green peas .......................... ½ cup
Vegetable stock or water ................ 3 cups
Corn flour ................................... 2 tblspns
Egg white ..................................... of 1 egg
Oil.......................................................... 1 tspn
Sweet corn niblets .................... 2 tblspns
Salt........................................................ to taste
Sugar ...................................................... a pinch
Crushed dried red chillies ............ ½ tspn

**METHOD OF PREPARATION**

1. Wash and cut mushrooms into four. Peel and cut carrots into one fourth inch pieces. Wash capsicum, halve, deseed and cut into one fourth inch pieces
2. Boil carrots and green peas in vegetable stock or water. Keep aside.
3. Dissolve corn flour in half a cup of water. Beat egg white lightly. Keep aside.
4. Heat oil, add capsicum and mushroom pieces and cook for two to three minutes on high heat.
5. Add warm vegetable stock or water along with carrots, green peas and sweet corn niblets, bring it to a boil. Add salt to taste, sugar and crushed red chillies.
6. Stir in corn flour dissolved in water, stirring continuously. Cook at boiling hot temperature for one minute.
7. Finally add the beaten egg white, stir lightly and serve hot.

**Chef's Tip:**

*If you are using whole fresh peas, do not throw away the peel. Instead use them as vegetable after removing and discarding thin inner layer.*

**NUTRITIONAL INFORMATION**

| Calories | Proteins | Fat | Carbohydrates | Fibre |
|---|---|---|---|---|
| 45 | 1.2 | 1.2 | 5.6 | 0.8 |

Fresh shelled green peas supply about 90-100 cals/100 gms. of weight. It has 7% protein and 72% moisture. Fresh green peas are a good source of complex carbohydrate i.e. fibre.

# THAI VEGETABLE
## *Soup*

### INGREDIENTS

Mushrooms ........................................ 10-12
Carrot ............................... 1 medium sized
Spring onions ......................2 small sized
Fresh coriander leaves ..................... 1/4 cup
Lettuce leaves .................................... 10-12
Dried red chillies ....................................... 3
Lemon juice ...................................... 1 tblspn
Lemon grass stalks ........2 one inch pieces
Vegetable stock or water ................ 3 cups
Bean sprouts ........................................ 3/4 cup
Salt ..................................................... to taste
Thin coconut milk ................................ 1 cup

### METHOD OF PREPARATION

1. Wash and slice mushrooms. Peel, wash and cut carrot into thin slices. Wash and finely chop spring onions including some of the greens. Wash and roughly chop fresh coriander leaves.
2. Wash and shred lettuce leaves. Wash, deseed and chop dried red chillies. Soak them in lemon juice. Wash and cut lemon grass stalks into big pieces.
3. Bring vegetable stock or water to a boil, add thinly sliced carrot and lemon grass. Cover and reduce heat, simmer for five minutes. Stir in sliced mushrooms, chopped spring onion, bean sprouts, shredded lettuce leaves and salt to taste. Bring it to a boil.
4. Add thin coconut milk, reduce heat, do not cover and stir in chopped dried red chillies soaked in lemon juice. Stir in roughly chopped fresh coriander leaves.
5. Serve piping hot.

### NUTRITIONAL INFORMATION

| Calories | Proteins | Fat | Carbohydrates | Fibre |
|---|---|---|---|---|
| 120 | 2. 5 | 8.4 | 9.3 | 0.8 |

Coconut milk though high in fat, can be skimmed and diluted to reduce the calorie count. Fresh coconut milk can be obtained by grinding one part grated coconut with two parts of warm water. Squeeze and strain through a muslin cloth. The alkaline properties present in the coconut milk help in reducing the stomach acidity.

# SPINACH
## *Soup*

### INGREDIENTS

Spinach ........................ 4 bundles
Onion ........................ 1 medium sized
Garlic ........................ 5 cloves
Oil ........................ 1 tblspn
Bay leaf ........................ 1
Pepper corns ........................ 6-8
Vegetable stock or water ........................ 3 cups
Cumin powder ........................ ½ tspn
Salt ........................ to taste
Pepper powder ........................ ½ tspn
Skimmed milk ........................ 1 cup

### METHOD OF PREPARATION

1. Clean spinach, wash thoroughly and roughly chop. Peel and chop onion and garlic.
2. Heat oil in a pan, add bay leaf, pepper corns and chopped garlic. Stir-fry briefly.
3. Add chopped onion and cook, stirring continuously until onion turns soft and translucent.
4. Add chopped spinach, continue to cook for three to four minutes. Cool the mixture.
5. Remove bay leaf and puree spinach to a fine consistency in a blender.
6. Bring vegetable stock or water to a boil, add spinach puree, cumin powder, salt and white pepper powder to taste. Mix well and let it simmer for a few minutes.
7. Stir in skimmed milk and simmer for two minutes. Serve hot.

### NUTRITIONAL INFORMATION

| Calories | Proteins | Fat | Carbohydrates | Fibre |
|---|---|---|---|---|
| 45 | 2.0 | 1.4 | 5.3 | 0.4 |

Spinach is one of the most commonly consumed green leafy vegetable. Like all leafy vegetables, spinach is low in calories. It is a rich source of iron, calcium, B-Carotene, B Complex and Vitamin C.

Addition of skimmed milk to soups enhances calcium and protein content of the dish.

# TOMATO EGG DROP

## *Soup*

### INGREDIENTS

Egg whites .................................. of 2 eggs
Corn flour .................................... 3 tblspns
Vegetable stock or water ................ 4 cups
Tomatoes ......................... 3 medium sized
Onion ............................... 1 medium sized
Garlic ............................................ 4 cloves
Ginger .................................... 1 inch knob
Fresh coriander leaves ..................... ¼ cup
Oil ........................................................ 1 tspn
Tomato ketchup ............................ 4 tblspns
Salt ................................................... to taste
White pepper powder ..................... to taste
White vinegar .................................... 2 tspns

### METHOD OF PREPARATION

1. Beat egg whites lightly. Dissolve corn flour in one fourth cup vegetable stock or water.
2. Wash and chop tomatoes finely. Peel and chop onion and garlic. Peel, wash and chop ginger finely. Clean, wash and chop fresh coriander leaves.
3. Heat oil, add chopped ginger and garlic and stir-fry for a half a minute.
4. Add chopped onion and continue to stir-fry till onions are soft and translucent.
5. Add tomato ketchup and chopped tomatoes. Cook for about five minutes.
6. Add stock or water, add salt and white pepper powder to taste and stir. Bring to a boil.
7. Add corn flour dissolved in vegetable stock or water, a little at a time stirring continuously till soup turns to a thick soup consistency. Add white vinegar and stir.
8. Pour the beaten egg white in a steady thin stream, while stirring lightly, allow it to coagulate and come on top.
9. Stir in chopped green coriander, reserve some for garnishing.
10. Serve hot immediately, garnished with chopped green coriander.

### NUTRITIONAL INFORMATION

| Calories | Proteins | Fat | Carbohydrates | Fibre |
|---|---|---|---|---|
| 35 | 2.0 | 1.1 | 6.0 | 0.4 |

Pepper ranks next to salt as the most common seasoning. The dried variety comes in two forms, white and black. Both come from the dried berries of the same tropical vine creeper. The difference is in processing. For white pepper, the outer dark surface of the tiny berries is rubbed off and only the inside is used. White pepper is also less pungent than black pepper.

Paprika is a mild member of the pepper family. It should be noted that pepper is even a greater stimulant than chillies. Those suffering from ulcer should not only avoid chillies, but also not use pepper for seasoning.

# VEGETABLE CLEAR

## *Soup*

### INGREDIENTS

Carrot ............................. 1 medium sized
Cabbage ............................. ¼ small
Tomato ............................. 1 medium sized
Capsicum ............................. 1 medium sized
Spinach ............................. 16-20 leaves
Garlic ............................. 3-4 cloves
Mushrooms ............................. 80 gms
Oil ............................. ½ tspn
Bean sprouts ............................. ½ cup
Vegetable stock or water ............................. 5 cups
Salt ............................. to taste
Lemon juice ............................. 1 tspn
Crushed pepper corns ............................. ½ tspn

### METHOD OF PREPARATION

1. Wash and peel carrot, cut into two lengthwise. Make thin slices.
2. Wash and dice cabbage into one cm. sized pieces. Wash tomato, cut into quarter, remove seeds and dice it into one cm. sized pieces. Wash, halve and deseed capsicum. Dice into one cm. sized pieces.
3. Clean spinach leaves, wash thoroughly and chop roughly. Peel and slice garlic. Wash and slice mushrooms.
4. Heat oil in a pan and add sliced garlic. Stir-fry briefly.
5. Add mushrooms, bean sprouts and all the vegetables except tomato. Stir in vegetable stock or water and salt to taste. Bring it to a boil and simmer for two minutes.
6. Add tomato pieces and stir in lemon juice and crushed pepper corn. Serve hot.

### NUTRITIONAL INFORMATION

| Calories | Proteins | Fat | Carbohydrates | Fibre |
|---|---|---|---|---|
| 60 | 3.3 | 0.5 | 9.5 | 1.6 |

Cabbage, a low caloric leafy vegetable, belongs to the cruciferous family like cauliflower, radish, turnip, brussel sprouts etc. There are wide varieties of cabbage. The regular or western variety is low in B-carotene and Vitamin C but the Chinese variety commonly called Chinese leaf is very high in both. Cabbage has fair amount of potassium and choline. Like other members of the cruciferous family, Chinese cabbage contains indols that are believed to fight cancer-producing cells.

But a word of caution. Cabbage also contains goitrogen, certain anti-thyroid substances, which interfere with iodine uptake by thyroid gland. Excessive intake of these foods in the face of marginal intake of iodine from foods and water, may lead to precipitation of goitre.

# SOUTHERN ITALIAN
## *Vegetable Soup*

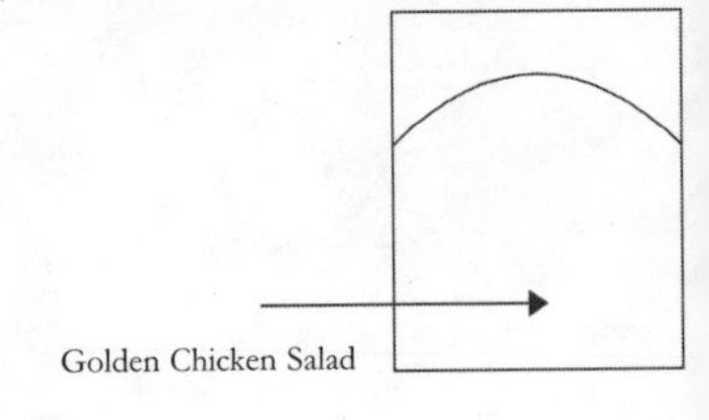
Golden Chicken Salad

### INGREDIENTS

Carrot ............ 1 medium sized
Potatoes ............ 2 medium sized
Cabbage ............ ¼ small sized
Tomatoes ............ 2 medium sized
Onion ............ 1 medium sized
Garlic ............ 4 cloves
Celery ............ 1 inch stalk
Fresh basil ............ 6-8 leaves
Olive oil ............ 1 tspn
Salt ............ to taste
White pepper powder ............ to taste
Macaroni ............ ¼ cup
Stock or water ............ 4 cups

### METHOD OF PREPARATION

1. Wash and peel the carrot and chop it into very small dices.
2. Peel potatoes, cut into very small dices and leave them in water.
3. Cut cabbage into very small dices.
4. Wash, remove the eye of the tomato and make a small incision at the bottom. Boil water and blanch the tomatoes for one to two minutes and remove immediately.
5. Peel, deseed and puree or mince the tomatoes.
6. Peel onion and garlic and chop as fine as possible. Wash and chop celery and basil leaves, reserve a few basil leaves for garnish.
7. Heat olive oil in a pan, add onion and garlic and sauté till they turn translucent.
8. Add celery, carrot and potato pieces. Stir continuously and cook for five minutes.
9. Add cabbage, tomatoes and cook stirring continuously. Add salt, white pepper powder, basil and the macaroni, stir and add stock or water and bring it to a boil.
10. Lower the flame and simmer till the vegetables are cooked and the soup has thickened.
11. Garnish with fresh basil.

**Chef's Concern:**

*Basil is known to emit ozone rather than oxygen that is emitted by other plants.*

### NUTRITIONAL INFORMATION

| Calories | Proteins | Fat | Carbohydrates | Fibre |
|---|---|---|---|---|
| 125 | 1.8 | 2.3 | 14.0 | 1.0 |

Exotic sweet basil comes from the same family as *tulsi*. *Tulsi* is used to treat fever, colds, flue, stomach cramps, vomiting, headaches and menstrual cramps. Its role in reducing cholesterol and triglycerides is also worth mentioning. *Tulsi* is worshipped in India.

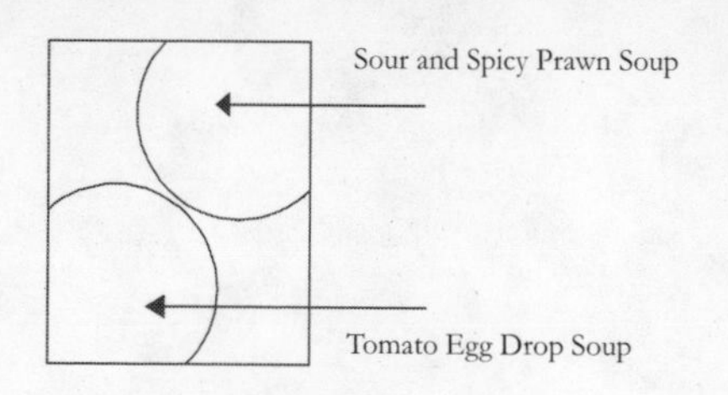


# SOUR AND SPICY PRAWN

## *Soup*

### INGREDIENTS

Prawns .................... 12-16 medium sized
Spring onion ................................2-3 small
Fresh mushrooms ................................. 6-8
Ginger ..................................... 1 inch knob
Lemon grass stalks ........2 one inch length
Kafir Lime leaves .......................... 3 leaves
Green chillies ........................................ 2
Fresh red chilli ........................................ 1
Fresh coriander leaves ..................... ¼ cup
Lemon rind ......................................... 1 tspn
Chicken stock .................................. 4 cups
Fish sauce (optional) ................... ½ tblspn
Lemon juice ................................. 2 tblspns
Salt ................................................. to taste

### METHOD OF PREPARATION

1. Shell and devein prawns and wash them thoroughly. Reserve shells.
2. Peel spring onion and coarsely chop. Wash and slice fresh mushrooms. Peel and slice ginger. Wash and roughly chop lemon grass. Wash kafir lime leaves.
3. Wash and roughly chop green chillies. Wash and cut fresh red chilli into slivers. Reserve for garnish. Wash and coarsely chop fresh coriander leaves.
4. Stir in prawn shells, sliced ginger, chopped green chillies, chopped lemon grass, lemon rind and Kafir lime leaves in chicken stock. Bring it to a boil, cover, reduce heat and simmer for fifteen minutes. Strain the mixture through a sieve and return the liquid to the saucepan. Bring it to a boil.
5. Add prawns and sliced mushrooms. Simmer for two to three minutes and stir in the fish sauce and lemon juice. Add salt to taste, stir and immediately remove from heat to prevent overcooking of prawns.
6. Serve piping hot, garnished with slivers of fresh chillies, chopped fresh coriander leaves and spring onion.

### NUTRITIONAL INFORMATION

| Calories | Proteins | Fat | Carbohydrates | Fibre |
|---|---|---|---|---|
| 95 | 19.2 | 1.0 | 2.6 | 0.1 |

Lemon grass has an exquisite citrusy and faintly gingery flavour. It is the keynote of South-East Asian cooking. In India, it is commonly used in household for flavouring tea and apart from its distinct flavour, lemon grass tea is considered good for cold. The Gujarati name for lemon grass is *Leeli Chai.*

# CHICKEN AND SWEET CORN

*Soup*

## INGREDIENTS

Egg whites .................................. of 2 eggs
Corn flour .................................. 1 tblspn
Chicken breasts, skinless & boneless ........ 2
Chicken stock or water.................. 4 cups
Sweet corn, cream style............100 gms
Salt .................................................. to taste
White pepper powder .................... to taste

## METHOD OF PREPARATION

1. Beat egg whites lightly and keep aside. Dissolve corn flour in half a cup of water.
2. Cut boneless chicken breasts into small pieces and cook in four cups of boiling chicken stock or water for five minutes.
3. Add sweet corn and continue to boil. Add salt and white pepper powder.
4. After about two minutes of boiling reduce the flame and then add corn flour dissolved in water. Stir continuously and bring to a boil again.
5. Add the beaten egg white, gently stir and serve hot.

## NUTRITIONAL INFORMATION

| Calories | Proteins | Fat | Carbohydrates | Fibre |
|---|---|---|---|---|
| 130 | 17.5 | 3.2 | 6.7 | 0.2 |

Sweet corn is a cereal and gives about 125-150 cals/100 gms. In tender form it has about 5% protein however it is suggested that corn based recipes should be supplemented with good quality protein foods. In this recipe it is worth noting that addition of chicken and egg white has improved the quality and quantity of the protein remarkably.

# TOMATO AND CARROT

*Soup*

## INGREDIENTS

| | | | |
|---|---|---|---|
| Onion | 1 medium sized | Vegetable stock or water | 2 cups |
| Garlic | 4 cloves | Bay leaf | 1 |
| Carrots | 2 medium sized | Pepper corns | 4-6 |
| Tomatoes | 8 medium sized | Fresh mint leaves | 4-6 |
| Potato | 1 medium sized | Salt | to taste |
| Brown bread | 2 slices | | |

## METHOD OF PREPARATION

1. Peel and slice onion. Peel garlic and crush lightly. Scrub and wash carrots and chop them roughly. Wash tomatoes and chop them roughly. Peel and roughly slice the potato.
2. Toast brown bread slices in a toaster and cut toasted slices with a sharp knife into small square pieces. Alternately you can first cut the bread slices into small pieces and then dry roast in a non-stick pan, tossing continuously, till they are crisp.
3. Pressure cook all the prepared vegetables including onion and garlic along with one cup vegetable stock or water, bay leaf, pepper corns, mint leaves and salt.
4. Cool the cooked mixture. Ensure that the potato is thoroughly cooked.
5. Remove bay leaf and then puree it to a fine consistency in a blender.
6. Heat the pureed vegetables in a pan, add the remaining vegetable stock or water and adjust seasoning. Simmer for five minutes and serve with toasted brown bread *croutons.*

### NUTRITIONAL INFORMATION

| Calories | Proteins | Fat | Carbohydrates | Fibre |
|---|---|---|---|---|
| 95 | 2.8 | 1.5 | 18.8 | 1.6 |

It is customary to serve fried croutons with soup. But have you thought about the fact that sometimes these croutons can supply more calories than the soup itself! Using toasted croutons made from whole wheat bread will not only be a healthy alternative to fried croutons, but also to bread-sticks (made from refined flour or maida) which are frequently served with soup.

# SNACKS

Foods that are eaten in-between meals or sometimes as a substitute to a meal or as 'fast foods' or foods from vending machines can all be referred to as 'snacks'. Changing life style, a busy, hectic schedule, socializing, and easy accessibility to ready-to-eat food has made 'snacking' important. Snacking can be a cause of concern when the snacks are high in sugar, salt and fat but low in micro-nutrients. However if planned well, snacks can be equally healthy to bridge the gap of nutrient requirement between two meals. Hence a snack which supplements a meal should be considered healthy.

Here are some instances where simple alterations can increase the nutrient content of snacks:

* Addition of pulses and lentils in cereal-based vegetarian snacks improves the protein quality remarkably as we have done in Paushtik Poha.

* It is a good practice to add some paneer in sandwiches etc. for improving calcium and protein. See recipe — Apple and Cheese Toast.

* In cutlets, instead of just having potato as a base, add carrot, spinach or *methi* too. These can give B-carotene, calcium and other nutrients.

* If you eat egg, coat cutlets with egg, it will give more protein.

* In *chiwda* add groundnut, sesame seeds, roasted *chana dal* for protein and calcium. It can be prepared in an iron *kadai* to increase the iron content. To limit the intake of fat, use roasted *dalmoth*, *chiwdas*, instead of fried.

* Serve snacks with chutney made from mint and coriander for extra Vitamin C, iron, B-carotene, calcium and B complex. New research shows that Tomato Ketchup may finally not be as bad after all because of the presence of lycopene in it. However check for preservatives and sodium content.

* Add bran and vegetables (carrot, spinach, *methi*, *karela* etc.) to *khakras* and *muthiyas* to increase the fibre content.

One should not over indulge in fried snacks, especially weight watchers, and those with cardiovascular diseases, diabetes and alike. Instead steamed, boiled snacks like *dhokla*, *muthiya*, *idlis* are good substitutes.

Foods like finger chips, burgers, cakes, cookies etc. are termed 'junk-food' as they are high in calories, fat and carbohydrates but very low in other nutrients. They are getting very popular with children, so it is a good idea to incorporate with them other foods that are nutrient dense. For example a burger bun can be made with whole wheat flour. Milk powder can also be added to increase the protein and calcium content. Cutlets can have spinach, carrot and other such vegetables instead of just potato or chicken or fish.

It is difficult to avoid snacking, but definitely we can make the snacks more nutritious and healthy. This section offers you a wide variety of lip-smacking, healthy snacks.

# CHATPATI

## *Tikki*

### INGREDIENTS

Raw bananas .................... 2 medium sized
Carrots ............................ 2 medium sized
Onion ............................... 1 medium sized
Ginger .................................... 1 inch knob
Green chillies ........................................ 3-4
Mint leaves ........................................... 8-10
Raisins ............................................... 15-20
Seedless dates ........................................... 6
Roasted peanuts without skin ........ ½ cup
Oil .................................................. 1 tspns
Mustard seeds ................................ ½ tspn
*Urad dal* ........................................... ½ tspn
Red chilli powder .......................... 1 tspns
*Chaat masala* powder ..................... 2 tspns
Salt ................................................. to taste
Lemon juice .................................. 2 tspns

### METHOD OF PREPARATION

1. Boil whole raw bananas in sufficient water for fifteen to twenty minutes. Cool, peel and mash well. Wash, peel and grate the carrot. Peel and finely chop onion and ginger.
2. Wash, remove stem and finely chop green chillies. Wash and finely chop mint leaves.
3. Wash raisins and roughly chop them with seedless dates. Divide this into twelve equal portions. Grind roasted peanuts to a coarse powder.
4. Heat oil in a non-stick pan and add mustard seeds, let them crackle and add *urad dal*. Let it cook till it starts turning brown. Add chopped onion, ginger, garlic and green chillies. Stir-fry for half a minute. Add red chilli powder, mix and quickly add grated carrot.
5. Cook over medium heat for two to three minutes. Sprinkle chopped mint leaves, *chaat masala* powder, mix well and remove from heat.
6. Cool and mix the cooked masala with the mashed raw banana. Add salt to taste, lemon juice and mix well.
7. Divide this mixture into twelve equal portions. Stuff a portion of the date and raisin mixture into each portion of raw banana mixture.
8. Wet your palm and form this mixture into a patty (*tikki*) of not more than half inch thickness.
9. Coat the *tikkis* with coarse peanut powder, pressing them lightly with your palms.
10. Heat a non-stick fry pan or a griddle plate (*tawa*), place the peanut coated *tikkis*. Cook on medium heat till the crust is crisp and nicely brown. Make sure that the *tikkis* are heated through.

### NUTRITIONAL INFORMATION

| Calories | Proteins | Fat | Carbohydrates | Fibre |
|---|---|---|---|---|
| 160 | 4.5 | 5.9 | 22.5 | 1.6 |

Raisins are dried grapes and are a good source of glucose, iron and phosphorous. Phosphorous is an important component of the nerve cells and plays a central role in energy metabolism. Raisins are an excellent natural laxative.

# ORIENTAL FISH
## *Kababs*

### INGREDIENTS

**For Kabab**

Fish fillet .......... 500 gms
Lemon juice .......... 1 tblspn
Fresh button mushrooms .......... 16
Fresh Lychees .......... 12
Black grapes (seedless) .......... 24
Oil .......... ½ tblspn

**For Sauce**

Ginger .......... 1 inch piece
Garlic .......... 2 cloves
Oil .......... 1 tblspn
Soya sauce .......... 2 tblspns
Crushed pepper corn .......... 1 tspn
Red wine (optional) .......... 2 tblspns
Honey .......... 2 tspns

### METHOD OF PREPARATION

1. Clean the fish and cut it into twenty four equal size cubes. Apply lemon juice and keep aside.
2. Wash and cut the stems of mushrooms. Sweat the trimmed mushrooms in a non-stick sauce pan on medium heat with a lid on for three to four minutes. Toss them occasionally. Remove, strain and keep the mushrooms aside and reserve the cooking liquor for the sauce.
3. Peel the lychees, halve, remove stone and keep. Wash the grapes and keep.
4. Peel, wash and finely chop the ginger. Peel and crush the garlic.
5. Heat oil in a small non-stick pan over moderate heat, add crushed garlic and chopped ginger to the pan and cook for fifteen seconds on medium heat. Add the soya sauce, crushed pepper corn, reserved cooking liquor, red wine and one fourth cup water and bring to boil. Add honey and mix well.
6. Lower the heat and simmer gently for two to three minutes. Remove and keep warm till the kababs are ready.
7. Skewer fish, cooked mushrooms, black grapes and lychees on to the wooden skewers.
8. Brush with the oil and grill for ten minutes, alternately cook it in a pre-heated oven (180 degrees Celsius) for ten to twelve or until the fish is tender. You can also cook this dish on a griddle plate or a thick pan. Use a non-stick pan for better results. Make sure to turn the skewers at regular intervals for even cooking.
9. Lace the kababs with the sauce and serve immediately.

**Chef's Tip:**

*Alternately you may cook fish fingers in a preheated oven or a griller.*

### NUTRITIONAL INFORMATION

| Calories | Proteins | Fat | Carbohydrates | Fibre |
|---|---|---|---|---|
| 285 | 22.0 | 7.4 | 10.7 | 0.5 |

Lychees are a favourite fruit of many. About ten lychees would about 60 cals. They also supply Vitamin C and potassium. Compared to other fruits they have a high amount of sodium. Hence those on low sodium diet should limit their consumption.

# PAUSHTIK

*Poha*

## INGREDIENTS

Pressed rice (*Poha*) .......................... 2 cups
Green chillies .......................................... 3
Onion ............................... 2 medium sized
Fresh coriander leaves .................... ¼ cup
Curry leaves ........................................ 8-10
Soya granules ................................... ½ cup
Oil ................................................. 1 tblspn
Cumin seeds ...................................... 1 tspn
Turmeric powder ............................ ½ tspn
Roasted peanuts ............................... ½ cup
Salt ................................................ to taste
Lemon juice .................................. 2 tblspns

## METHOD OF PREPARATION

1. Take *poha* in a colander, pour three to four cups of water evenly to moisten them. Drain well. Wash, remove stem and chop green chillies. Peel and chop onion. Wash and chop coriander leaves. Wash curry leaves and pat dry.
2. Wash soya granules with warm water or alternately soak it in one cup water for fifteen to twenty minutes. Drain and keep aside.
3. Heat oil in a non-stick pan and add cumin seeds. Stir-fry briefly. Add chopped green chillies, curry leaves, turmeric powder and chopped onion. Stir-fry for two minutes on medium heat. Add soya granules and sprinkle quarter cup water on it. Cook covered on low heat for five minutes. Stir well.
4. Add *poha* and toss over medium flame till it is heated through. Add roasted peanuts, salt and lemon juice. Toss well.
5. Serve hot immediately garnished with chopped coriander leaves.

### NUTRITIONAL INFORMATION

| Calories | Proteins | Fat | Carbohydrates | Fibre |
|---|---|---|---|---|
| 185 | 5.1 | 4.0 | 29.3 | 0.3 |

Rice has only 0.7% of iron, however, the method of processing rice to *poha*, which involves the use of iron vessels (such as *kadai*), results in an increase of iron upto 20%. Addition of soya or soya products can remarkably improve the quantity and quality of protein.

# APPLE AND CHEESE
## *Toast*

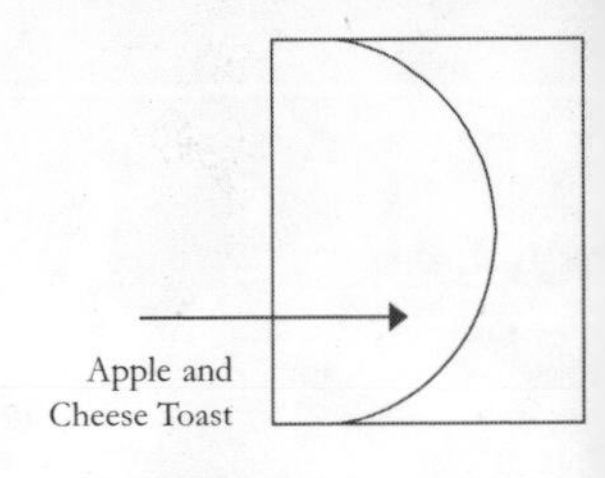


### INGREDIENTS

Apples .................................. 2 large sized
Lemon juice ................................ 1 tblspn
Cashew nuts ............................................ 8
Orange juice .................................... ½ cup
Whole meal bread ........................ 4 slices
Low-fat cottage cheese .............. 120 gms
Cinnamon powder ........................... ½ tspn
Honey ........................................... 1 tblspn

### METHOD OF PREPARATION

1. Peel, core and cut the apples into thick slices. Sprinkle lemon juice on apple slices.
2. Toast the cashew nuts in a pan or in a preheated oven till light golden, cool and crush coarsely.
3. Heat a non-stick pan and gently poach the apple slices in the orange juice for about ten minutes or until just soft, turn them over carefully for even cooking.
4. Toast the bread slices, trim the sides.
5. Grate the cottage cheese and mix with the crushed cashew nuts thoroughly.
6. Spread this mixture on the toasted bread slice and arrange the cooked apple slices on top.
7. Sprinkle cinnamon powder and place under a hot grill or in a preheated oven (180 degree Celsius) until browned to light golden.
8. Drizzle the honey on the hot toasts, cut to desired shape and serve.

### NUTRITIONAL INFORMATION

| Calories | Proteins | Fat | Carbohydrates | Fibre |
|---|---|---|---|---|
| 200 | 10.4 | 7.1 | 22.0 | 0.6 |

Honey, considered a holy food, contains iron, phosphorous, calcium, sodium, potassium, sulphur and manganese. It is used as a base for many Ayurvedic medicines. It is known to benefit patients with constipation, cold and cough.

A word of caution, when honey is to be fed to infants— honey has been identified as a food source of certain bacteria (Clostridium botulinum), which can result in diahorrea. These spores are extremely resistant to heat treatment and are not easily destroyed by present methods of processing honey.

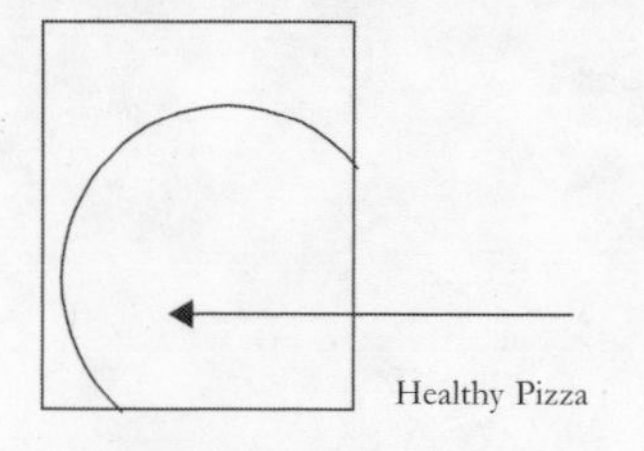

Healthy Pizza

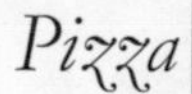

# HEALTHY *Pizza*

## INGREDIENTS

**For pizza base**

Dried yeast ................................ 1 ½ tspn
Sugar ........................................ 1 tspn
Whole meal flour ..................... 1 ½ cups
Soya flour .................................. 2 tblspns
Salt ............................................. 1 tspn
Olive oil .......................................1 tblspn
Wheat bran ................................ 2 tblspns

**For Sauce**

Tomatoes ..........................4 medium size
Onion ...................................... 1 small size
Garlic ........................................... 4-5 cloves
Fresh basil ............................ a few leaves
Olive oil ............................................2 tblspn
Salt ................................................. to taste
Crushed dried red chillies ........... 1 tspn

**For Topping**

Mushrooms ...................................... 10-12
Capsicum ................................... 1 medium
Tomatoes ...................... 2 medium sized
Onion ........................... 1 medium sized
Low fat Mozzarella cheese ....... 1 tblspn
Oregano (dried) ............................ ¼ tspn

## METHOD OF PREPARATION

1. Mix yeast with sugar and one teaspoon warm water and leave aside until frothy.
2. Add frothy yeast to a mixture of whole meal and soya flour. Add salt, olive oil and wheat bran. Add water and knead into soft dough.
3. Leave the dough covered with a damp cloth in a warm place for about forty five minutes or until the dough is about double in volume.
4. Divide pizza dough into four, roll out each portion into medium thick eight inch disc. Prick them with a fork all over. Preheat an oven to 220 degree Celsius.
5. For the sauce, wash and chop tomatoes finely. Peel and chop onion and garlic. Wash and tear basil leaves into small pieces. Heat olive oil in a pan, add chopped onion and garlic, stir-fry briefly and add chopped tomatoes. Add one cup of water and bring it to a boil. Stir in the basil leaves, salt and crushed dried red chillies. Simmer for about five minutes on medium heat or till it reaches thick dropping consistency.
6. For pizza topping, wash mushrooms thoroughly with plenty of water, pat them dry and slice. Wash capsicum, halve to deseed and then cut into thin strips. Wash and cut tomatoes to quarter and cut into thin strips. Peel and slice onion. Grate low-fat mozzarella cheese.
7. Spread prepared pizza sauce on rolled pizza base, top it with sliced onion, sliced mushrooms, tomato and capsicum strips. Finally sprinkle grated low-fat mozzarella cheese to evenly cover the pizza top. Crush dried oregano leaves and sprinkle on the pizza.

8. Place it on greased ovenproof tray and bake in a preheated oven for about twenty minutes or until the pizza base is crisp and the cheese melts and starts bubbling.
9. Remove from oven, cut into six or eight pieces and serve hot.

(For a medium size Pizza)

Nutrient Comparison of Healthy vs. Regular Pizza (one piece)

| Calorie | Protein | Fat | Carbohydrates | Fibre |
|---|---|---|---|---|
| Healthy Pizza 100-125 | 4.0 | 2.2 | 15.0 | 1.0 |
| Regular Pizza 175-200 | 4.0 | 6.0 | 28.0 | 0.2 |

**Chef's Tip:**

*The pizza base can be baked in advance separately and then bake it again with the topping on it at the time of consumption.*

## NUTRITIONAL INFORMATION

| Calories | Proteins | Fat | Carbohydrates | Fibre |
|---|---|---|---|---|
| 385 | 13.0 | 9.5 | 64.0 | 3.0 |

The regular pizzas that we eat have the base made up of refined flour (*maida*). This supplies more calories with very few other nutrients. This pizza cannot be recommended for weight watchers or diabetics. In contrast to this, the base in this recipe is made from whole wheat flour and soya flour, to which bran is also added. Compared to *maida*, whole-wheat flour or *atta* has more thiamin, riboflavin, niacin and iron. Soya flour gives us a good amount of protein. Addition of wheat bran not only increases fibre but also adds to the nutritional value of the whole dish.

Also note the use of low-fat cheese in the recipe.

# SPICED EGGPLANT

*Savoury*

## INGREDIENTS

Eggplant
.......... 1 medium sized (approx. 250 gms)
Garlic .......................................... 5 cloves
Tomatoes ........................ 3 medium sized
Onion.............................. 1 medium sized
Green chillies ..................................... 2-3

Mint leaves ......................................... ¼ cup
Fresh coriander leaves .................... ¼ cup
Lemon juice ..................................... 1 tspn
Salt ................................................ to taste
Oil .................................................... 1 tspn
Brown bread ................................. 4 slices

## METHOD OF PREPARATION

1. Wash eggplant, prick it using a fork.
2. Roast eggplant over direct flame or in a pre heated oven until soft. Cool roasted eggplant, then remove the outer burnt skin completely. Wash it well. Drain excess water and chop it fine.
3. Peel and chop garlic. Wash and chop tomatoes. Peel and chop onion. Wash green chillies, remove stem and then chop. Clean, wash mint and fresh coriander leaves and chop them fine.
4. Mix chopped eggplants with chopped onion, chopped tomato, chopped garlic, chopped green chillies, chopped fresh coriander leaves, lemon juice and salt.
5. Cook this mixture in a non-stick pan with a little oil on medium heat until it dries well.
6. Toast brown bread slices till crisp. Spread this mixture on the toasted bread pieces. Sprinkle chopped mint leaves on top, cut each slice in two or four pieces. Serve warm, chilled or at room temperature.

**Chef's Tip:**

*To make it more delicious, grated low-fat mozzarella can be put on top and then put in hot oven until cheese melts and starts bubbling.*

## NUTRITIONAL INFORMATION

| Calories | Proteins | Fat | Carbohydrates | Fibre |
|---|---|---|---|---|
| 90 | 3.5 | 1.6 | 17.0 | 1.5 |

Eggplant or brinjal is a low calorie vegetable and a good source of phosphorous and iron. It has a fair amount of riboflavin, folic acid, choline and potassium.

Using whole wheat bread makes this recipe more nutrient dense. This feast is a healthy alternative to normal sandwiches.

# STEAMED

## *Crescents*

### INGREDIENTS

Rice flour .......... 1 cup
Salt .......... 1 tspn
Oil .......... 1 tspn

**Filling**

Carrot .......... 1 medium sized
Onion .......... 1 medium sized
Garlic .......... 6-8 cloves
Ginger .......... 1 inch knob
Green Chillies .......... 4-5
Capsicum .......... 1 medium sized
Roasted *chana dal* .......... ¼ cup
Oil .......... 1 tblspn
Cumin seeds .......... ½ tspn
*Kalonji* .......... ½ tspn
*Amchur* .......... 1 tspn
Salt .......... to taste

### METHOD OF PREPARATION

*Chef's Tip:*

*This recipe takes some practice to perfect it. Try once or twice before including this dish in the menu for invited guests.*

1. Peel, wash and grate the carrot. Peel and chop the onion, garlic and ginger as fine as possible. Wash and chop the green chillies. Wash capsicum, halve, deseed and chop it fine. Crush roasted *chana dal* lightly.
2. Heat oil in a non-stick pan, add cumin seeds and *kalonji*. Stir-fry briefly. Add chopped onion, garlic, ginger and green chillies and sauté for three to four minutes.
3. Add chopped capsicum and grated carrot and continue cooking. Add crushed *chana dal*, *amchur* and salt to taste. Remove, from heat and cool.
4. Bring one cup water to boil in a thick-bottomed non-stick pan. Add one teaspoon salt and oil. When the water starts boiling, add rice flour in a continuous flow, stirring rapidly to avoid lumps. Cook briefly, stirring all along.
5. Remove on to a plate, cover with a damp cloth and let it sweat for a few minutes. Knead with your palm to a smooth dough, cover and keep.
6. Divide the rice dough into sixteen to eighteen equal portions and make them into balls.
7. Lightly oil your palm and spread each ball to approximately three inches round disc, by pressing with your fingers to make it as thin as possible. Place sufficient filling and fold into half moon shape. Press the edges firmly with your fingers to seal. Repeat with the rest of the dough.
8. Heat water in steam pot and steam vegetable crescents in small batches for about ten to twelve minutes or till completely cooked.
9. Serve straight from the steamer with a hot and spicy sauce of your choice.

### NUTRITIONAL INFORMATION

| Calories | Proteins | Fat | Carbohydrates | Fibre |
|---|---|---|---|---|
| 265 | 4.9 | 5.0 | 48.0 | 0.7 |

Ginger is one of the best home remedies to cure nausea and vomiting. It is said to warm the center (stomach), aid digestion and assimilation, relieve cold spasms and cramps. It promotes menses. It is one of the most widely beneficial warming stimulants.

# SPINACH AND MUSHROOM

## *Pancakes*

### INGREDIENTS

Spinach leaves .............2 medium bundles
Onion ............................... 1 medium sized
Garlic ......................................... 6-8 cloves
Fresh mushrooms ........................ 100 gms
Oil .................................................... 1 tspn
Salt ................................................. to taste
White pepper powder .................... ¼ tspn
Whole wheat flour (*Atta*) ............. ¾ cup
Skimmed milk ................................. ¾ cup
*Ajwain* ............................................. ¼ tspn

### METHOD OF PREPARATION

1. Clean and wash the spinach leaves thoroughly. Drain and chop roughly.
2. Peel and chop onions. Peel and chop garlic. Wash and wipe mushrooms with a kitchen towel and chop them.
3. Heat oil in a pan, add chopped garlic, stir-fry briefly. Add chopped onion and mushrooms and cook till onion becomes soft and translucent. Cook on high heat so that the excess moisture from onions and mushrooms dries to some extent.
4. Add chopped spinach, add salt and white pepper powder, and then cook spinach until all the moisture evaporates. Remove from fire and divide the spinach mixture into eight equal portions and keep warm.
5. Mix salt with whole wheat flour and add milk. Whisk well. Add water as required, to make a smooth batter of pouring consistency. Strain the batter if there are lumps.
6. Mix in the *ajwain* and stir well. Rest the batter for at least fifteen minutes.
7. Heat a six inch non-stick pan. Grease with a little oil, if required. Pour half a ladle of batter and spread into a round shape. Cook for half a minute on medium heat, turn over and cook slightly.
8. Spread a portion of cooked spinach on three fourth portion of the pancake and then roll it ensuring that the filling does not spill out.
9. Cook rest of the pancakes in similar way. Serve immediately.

**Chef's Tip:**

*The pancakes can be topped with a little low fat cheese and gratinated in a grill just before serving.*

### NUTRITIONAL INFORMATION

| Calories | Proteins | Fat | Carbohydrates | Fibre |
|---|---|---|---|---|
| 150 | 7.0 | 2.3 | 25.4 | 1.3 |

Mushrooms have a lot of health benefit. They are a perfect alternative to meat not only because of their rich and succulent taste, but they are also low in calories, fat and cholesterol free, rich in vitamins and minerals.

Some types of mushroom are rich in protein, fibre, Vitamin B complex and minerals like calcium, magnesium, potassium, phosphorus and zinc.

Research in Japan confirms that mushroom lowers serum cholesterol and treats blood pressure, chronic fatigue and infection in general.

# GRILLED FISH
## *Fingers*

> **Chef's Tip:**
> *Alternately you may cook fish fingers in a preheated oven or a griller.*

### INGREDIENTS

| | | | |
|---|---|---|---|
| Fish fillet | 400 gms | White pepper powder | to taste |
| Lemon juice | 3 tblspns | Dried thyme | a pinch |
| Orange juice | 4 tblspns | Worcestershire sauce | 1 tblspn |
| Salt | to taste | Whole meal flour (*Atta*) | ½ cup |
| Mustard paste | ½ tspn | Oil | 1 tblspn |

### METHOD OF PREPARATION

1. Clean, wash and cut fish fillet into finger sized pieces. Pat dry with a clean and absorbent kitchen towel.
2. Combine lemon juice, orange juice, salt to taste, mustard paste, white pepper powder, dried thyme and Worcestershire sauce thoroughly.
3. Mix the fish fingers in above marinade. Refrigerate the marinated fish fingers for about fifteen to twenty minutes.
4. Season whole meal flour with salt and white pepper powder.
5. Roll marinated fish fingers in seasoned whole meal flour. Shake the excess flour off.
6. Heat a non-stick *tawa*, slightly grease with a few drops of oil.
7. Place the fish fingers on it. Cook on medium heat, turning it occasionally for uniform cooking and colour. Cook till golden brown in colour.

### NUTRITIONAL INFORMATION

| Calories | Proteins | Fat | Carbohydrates | Fibre |
|---|---|---|---|---|
| 205 | 15.6 | 4.9 | 7.8 | 0.1 |

Thyme is a favourite herb of many chefs. It not only improves taste and aroma of the dish but is also used for acute and chronic respiratory infections, fevers and digestive problems.

# TEX MEX CHICKEN

## *Wings*

### INGREDIENTS

Chicken wings .................................. 12-16
Garlic ......................................... 5-6 cloves
Celery ......................................... 2 inch stem
Oil ............................................ 1 tblspn
Bay leaf ....................................... 1
Brown sugar .................................... 1 tblspn
Malt vinegar ................................... 2 tblspns
Worcestershire sauce ........................... 2 tblspns
Tomato puree ................................... ¼ cup
Tomato ketchup ................................. ¼ cup
Red chilli powder .............................. 1 ½ tspn
Crushed pepper corn ............................ ½ tspn
Salt ........................................... to taste

### METHOD OF PREPARATION

1. Clean, wash and remove skin from chicken wings. Pat them dry with a clean and absorbent kitchen towel.
2. Peel and pound garlic along with washed celery stem to a paste.
3. Mix rest of the ingredients with the garlic and celery paste and marinate the wings for about one to two hours.
4. Preheat the oven to 200 degrees Celsius. Remove bay leaf from the marinade. Arrange chicken wings on the grilling tray of the oven. Ensure that the wings are placed in uniform pattern to ensure proper cooking.
5. Cook for fifteen to twenty minutes at 200 degrees Celsius. Turn over the wings a couple of times, basting it with the remaining marinade.
6. Cook till it is crisp from outside, but soft and tender inside.
7. Serve hot straight from the oven.

**Chef's Tip:**

*To preserve natural colour of green vegetables, cook them uncovered and do not overcook green vegetables. and do not add any baking soda.*

### NUTRITIONAL INFORMATION

| Calories | Proteins | Fat | Carbohydrates | Fibre |
|---|---|---|---|---|
| 130 | 17.6 | 4.6 | 3.2 | 0.1 |

It is a common practice to eat chicken wings with their skin. Chicken skin contains 25%-30% fat. To reduce the calorie content, it is recommended that chicken wings be used without skin and grilled, rather than fried.

# TANGDI
## *Kabab*

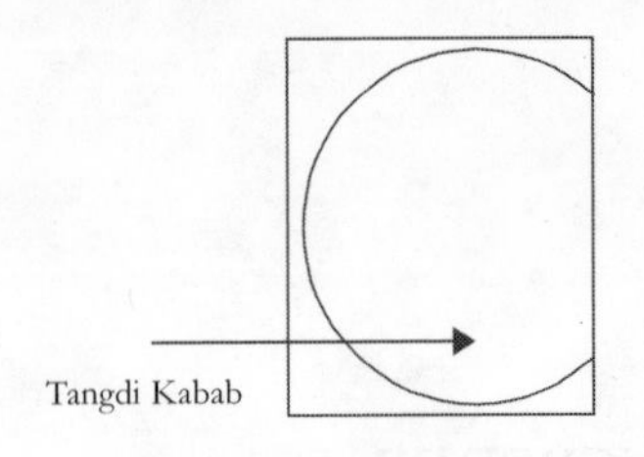
Tangdi Kabab

### INGREDIENTS

Chicken drumsticks
(Chicken legs without thigh section) ....... 8
Lemon juice .................................. 1 tblspn
Ginger ............................. 1 one inch knob
Garlic .......................................... 6 cloves
Green chillies ...................................... 4-6
Skimmed milk yogurt ....................... 1 cup
Gram flour (*Besan*) ...................... 2 tblspns
Turmeric powder ............................ 1 tbspn
*Garam masala* powder ...................... 1 tspn
Red chilli powder ............................. 1 tspn
*Chaat masala* powder ....................... 1 tspn
Lemon wedges ................. for garnishing
Salt .................................................. to taste

### METHOD OF PREPARATION

1. Clean and trim excess fat and skin from the drumsticks. Dry them with a clean and absorbent kitchen towel. Make three to four long deep incisions. Apply lemon juice and keep aside.
2. Peel ginger and garlic, wash and grind them to a paste.
3. Wash green chillies, remove stem and then chop them fine.
4. Hang skimmed milk yogurt for fifteen to twenty minutes to drain off excess water.
5. Roast gram flour in a non-stick pan on a low heat, stirring continuously. Cool and mix with hung yogurt, ginger and garlic paste, turmeric powder, *garam masala* powder, red chilli powder, salt and chopped green chillies.
6. Marinate chicken drumsticks in above mixture and refrigerate for one to two hours.
7. Skewer marinated chicken drumsticks and roast in a moderately hot charcoal fired tandoor or alternately cook in pre-heated oven at 220 degrees Celsius for five minutes. Reduce oven temperature to 180 degrees Celsius and further cook for fifteen to twenty minutes or till completely cooked. Turn drumsticks couple of times to ensure even cooking and colour.
8. Serve hot, sprinkled with *chaat masala* and lemon wedges.

### NUTRITIONAL INFORMATION

| Calories | Proteins | Fat | Carbohydrates | Fibre |
|---|---|---|---|---|
| 190 | 26.0 | 4.6 | 10.1 | 0.1 |

The flour of pulses like bengal gram(*Besan*) and others have starch, which is insoluble in cold water and must be cooked. Cooking causes granules to swell and the mixture thickens. It also softens and ruptures the cell to make starch granules available for the enzymatic digestive process in the intestine.

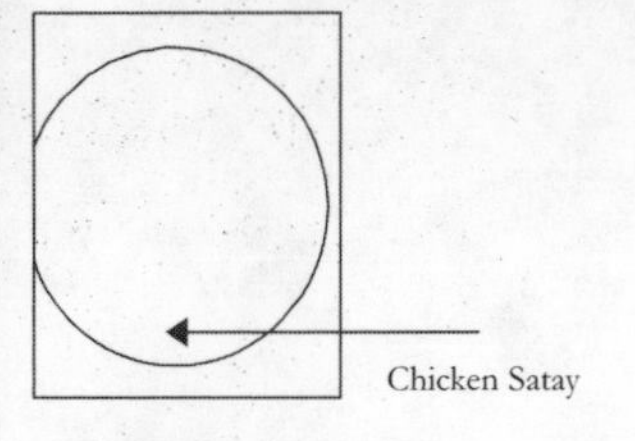
Chicken Satay

# CHICKEN
## *Satay*

### INGREDIENTS

Chicken breasts, skinless & boneless ........ 4 medium sized

**For Marination**

Lemon juice ........ 2 tblspns
Dark soya sauce ........ 1 tblspn
Oil ........ 1 tspn
Red chilli powder ........ 1 tspn
Salt ........ to taste

**For Sauce**

Onion ........ one small sized
Garlic ........ 4 cloves
Roasted peanut ........ ¼ cup
Oil ........ 1 tspn
Red chilli powder ........ ½ tspn
Dark soya sauce ........ 1 tblspn
Tomato puree ........ 3 tblspns
Honey ........ 2 tspns
Salt ........ to taste

### METHOD OF PREPARATION

1. Clean chicken breasts, wash them and then cut each into half-inch broad strips. Slightly flatten these long chicken strips.
2. Mix all the marinade ingredients thoroughly, add flattened chicken strips to it and leave aside for an hour.
3. Thread marinated flattened chicken strips equally onto eight inch long wooden skewers.
4. Heat a non-stick flat *tawa*, grease it slightly with a few drops of oil and place skewered chicken, a few at a time. Cook on high heat, turning them frequently. Cook for about three to four minutes or till they are just cooked.
5. Alternately cook in a preheated grill for ten to twelve minutes or until done, turning them couple of times.
6. Meanwhile prepare the sauce by peeling and grating onion. Peel and chop garlic. Crush roasted and peeled peanuts to a coarse powder.
7. Heat oil in a pan, add chopped garlic and grated onion. Cook on high heat, stirring continuously, for half a minute.
8. Add red chilli powder and then immediately add dark soya sauce, tomato puree, honey, crushed roasted peanuts, salt and one cup of water.
9. Bring it to a boil and simmer for five minutes, stirring occasionally.
10. Serve chicken satay accompanied with peanut sauce.

**Chef's Tip:**

*Soak wooden skewers in water for half an hour, prior to cooking, to avoid the skewer from burning while cooking.*

### NUTRITIONAL INFORMATION

| Calories | Proteins | Fat | Carbohydrates | Fibre |
|---|---|---|---|---|
| 155 | 17 | 6.8 | 3.7 | 0.2 |

Peanuts, rich in protein, are a concentrated source of energy, contain high level of B complex, especially thiamin and niacin. Oil seeds, particularly groundnut, get affected with fungi if they are not dried properly. This fungus produces some toxins like aflatoxin, which can harm liver and are known as carcinogens (cancer producing). It is thus necessary that only clean and properly dried groundnuts should be used.

# CHICKEN FLOWER

## *Dumpling*

### INGREDIENTS

| | | | |
|---|---|---|---|
| Basmati rice | ¾ cup | Chicken mince | 300 gms |
| Green chillies | 2-3 | Salt | to taste |
| Ginger | 1 inch knob | Crushed pepper corn | 1 tspn |

### METHOD OF PREPARATION

1. Pick, wash and soak rice in water for twenty minutes. Drain and keep aside.
2. Wash green chillies, remove stem and chop them fine.
3. Peel and wash ginger. Grind ginger into a fine paste.
4. Mix chicken mince with chopped green chillies, ginger paste, salt and crushed pepper corn. Divide this mixture into twelve equal portions.
5. Form round balls from each portion of chicken mix and then roll them in presoaked rice.
6. Place rice rolled chicken balls on a perforated rack which can be fitted into a steamer pot.
7. Boil water in the steamer pot and place the perforated rack in it. Cover the pot.
8. Steam for about fifteen to twenty minutes or until cooked.
9. Remove gently and serve hot with a dip of your choice.

**Chef's Tip:**

*Chicken Flower Dumplings are made best with chicken mince that is extra fine, preferably from chicken breast only.*

### NUTRITIONAL INFORMATION

| Calories | Proteins | Fat | Carbohydrates | Fibre |
|---|---|---|---|---|
| 175 | 23.0 | 4.4 | 8.0 | 0.1 |

Steaming is a healthy alternative in cooking especially for those who need to limit fat intake. Always look for snacks that are steamed rather than grilled or fried, since as a normal practice, a little fat is invariably used for grilling as well.

Steaming should be preferred over boiling also, because as compared to boiling, the loss of water-soluble nutrients (Vitamin C, B complex Vitamins, and a wide range of minerals) is minimum.

Vegetables are nature's gift to man and are an essential part of our diet. They not only add to the taste and palatability of a meal but also play a vital role in human nutrition by providing some of the important nutrients like Vitamins, minerals and fiber. Besides, vegetables have a key role in neutralizing the acid produced during digestion of protein-rich and fatty foods. The large amount of roughage provided by vegetables promotes digestion and helps in preventing constipation.

Vegetables are generally classified as leafy vegetables, roots and tubers and other vegetables. Some of the vegetables like potato, tapioca, sweet potato, yam are rich in carbohydrates. Peas and double beans are a good source of proteins. All dark, green, leafy vegetables are a rich source of B-carotene and Vitamin C. Leafy vegetables also provide a good amount of minerals like iron, calcium, potassium, magnesium etc. Peas, broad beans, tomatoes (ripe), garlic and greens provide B complex Vitamins. The daily requirement of some of the essential nutrients like Vitamins and minerals can be very well met by consuming 40-100 gms. of green leafy vegetables, 60-100 gms. of other vegetables as suggested by the Indian Council of Medical Research (ICMR) committee on Recommended Dietary Allowances (RDA).

India is one of largest producer of vegetables worldwide, however extensive studies show that the consumption is much lower than the recommended allowance. Hence there is a need to encourage each member of the family to eat vegetables in plenty. The recipes in this section provide you with a wide choice of tasty, healthy preparations to choose from.

Last but not the least, some health tips to be remembered while cooking vegetables:

* Wash vegetables well before cooking to get rid of any insecticide that may still be there. They should be not soaked in water, but cleaned under running water. If soaked, some of the Vitamins and minerals may be lost.
* Care should be taken to scrape or peel off as little of the vegetables as possible. This is because most of the minerals and Vitamins will be present in the layers immediately below the outer skin. Vegetables such as potatoes should be cooked with the skin on. The skin can be peeled later.
* Vegetables should be cut into large pieces to minimize nutrient loss.
* Over-cooking should be avoided, to prevent loss of important nutrients and it also helps to retain he the natural colour and flavour of vegetables. Do not add cooking soda to retain colour while cooking green vegetables.
* Any extra water left after cooking should be added to soups or other liquid preparations.

# CARROT AND ONION

## *Florentine*

### INGREDIENTS

| | | | |
|---|---|---|---|
| Fresh spinach | 2-3 medium sized bundles | Oil | 1 tspn |
| Cornflour | 2 tblspns | Salt | to taste |
| Carrots | 3-4 medium sized | White pepper powder | to taste |
| Broad beans (*Papdi*) | 100 gms | Skimmed milk | 2 cups |
| Onions | 2 medium sized | Mixed herbs (dried) | ¼ tspn |
| Garlic | 6-7 cloves | Fresh brown bread crumbs | ¼ cup |

### METHOD OF PREPARATION

1. Clean, trim and thoroughly wash the spinach in running water. Drain and finely chop the spinach. Dissolve the cornflour in quarter cup water.
2. Wash, peel and cut carrots into one and a half cm. sized cubes. Wash, string and cut broad beans into one and a half cm. sized pieces. Peel and thinly slice the onion. Peel garlic and crush them lightly.
3. Heat oil in a non-stick pan, add half the quantity of crushed garlic, stir briefly and add the chopped spinach. Sauté for four to five minutes over high heat, stirring occasionally or until the spinach is cooked completely. Add salt and white pepper powder to taste, stir well and remove from fire.
4. Heat the skimmed milk in a saucepan and bring to boil.
5. Add the remaining crushed garlic, carrots and broad beans and sliced onion. Cover and simmer for three to four minutes, stirring frequently. Add salt and white pepper powder to taste.
6. Gradually add the dissolved cornflour, stirring continuously, till it has a fairly thick sauce-like consistency. Sprinkle the mixed herb, stir well and remove from fire and keep warm.
7. Take an ovenproof glass or a ceramic dish and layer the cooked spinach. Pour the cooked vegetables along with the sauce over the spinach and level it with a spatula.
8. Sprinkle the fresh breadcrumbs on top of vegetables and bake in a preheated oven at 180 degree Celsius for ten minutes.

### NUTRITIONAL INFORMATION

| Calories | Proteins | Fat | Carbohydrates | Fibre |
|---|---|---|---|---|
| 110 | 6.3 | 1.6 | 19.6 | 1.1 |

One of the important nutrients spinach supplies is iron. In a vegetarian diet, leafy vegetables form an important source of iron. Inclusion of about fifty gms. of green leafy vegetables in our daily diets, can meet a fair proportion of iron needs besides providing calcium, B-carotene and Vitamin C. Iron is an essential element for the formation of hemoglobin. A lack of iron in diet results in anemia. Iron is also present in organ meat like liver and eggs. While consuming iron rich foods, especially from vegetarian sources, iron is best absorbed when eaten with Vitamin C and protein rich foods.

# CAULIFLOWER
## *Santa Fe*

### INGREDIENTS

| | | | |
|---|---|---|---|
| Cauliflower | 1 medium sized | Oil | 1 tblspn |
| Onions | 2 medium sized | Salt | to taste |
| Garlic | 5 cloves | Sweet corn, cream style | ¾ cup |
| Tomatoes | 4-5 medium sized | Pickled jalapeno peppers | 3-4 |
| Dried whole red chilli | 1 | Brown bread crumbs | ½ cup |

### METHOD OF PREPARATION

1. Separate cauliflower into small florets. Soak in salted water for fifteen minutes. Drain and refresh in cold water. Drain and keep aside.
2. Peel and chop onions and garlic. Wash and puree tomatoes in a blender. Remove stems and coarsely grind the dried red chillies. Roughly chop pickled Jalapeno peppers.
3. Heat oil in a non-stick pan, add chopped onion and stir-fry till onions becomes soft and translucent.
4. Add chopped garlic and stir-fry briefly. Add washed cauliflower florets and half a cup of water. Cover and cook on medium heat for ten minutes, stirring occasionally.
5. Add pureed tomato, coarsely ground red chillies and salt to taste. Cover and cook on medium heat for five to six minutes, stirring occasionally. Stir in cream style sweet corn and pickled jalapeno peppers.
6. Remove from heat, pour into an ovenproof dish, and sprinkle brown bread crumbs on top.
7. Place in a preheated oven at 180 degrees Celsius and bake for ten minutes. Serve hot.

***Chef's Tip:***

*Jalapeno (pronounced halapeno) peppers can be replaced with green chillies of thick variety that is not too hot.*

### NUTRITIONAL INFORMATION

| Calories | Proteins | Fat | Carbohydrates | Fibre |
|---|---|---|---|---|
| 125 | 5 | 4.5 | 16.3 | 2.2 |

Cauliflower, a moderate calorie vegetable, gives fair amount of minerals and Vitamins. Research has shown that vegetables from the cruciferous family (cauliflower, broccoli and brussels sprouts) contain a compound which can stimulate the production of cancer fighting enzymes in the body. Cauliflower also contains a good amount of Vitamin C, potassium and fibre.

# DAHI

## *Bhindi*

### INGREDIENTS

Tender lady fingers (*Bhindi*) .......... 400 gms
Green chillies .......................................... 3-4
Ginger .................................... 1 inch knob
Pepper corns .................................. ½ tspn
Skimmed milk yogurt..................... 1½ cup
Bengal gram flour (*Besan*) .......... 1 tblspn
Oil .................................................. 1½ tspn
Dried whole red chillies .......................... 2
Cumin seeds ...................................... 1 tspn
Coriander powder ......................... 1 tblspn
Turmeric powder ............................. ½ tspn
Salt ................................................. to taste

### METHOD OF PREPARATION

1. Select tender and small lady fingers. Wash and wipe them dry with a clean and absorbent kitchen towel.
2. Trim the stem and the tip. Wash green chillies, remove stem and then slit them.
3. Peel, wash and grind ginger with pepper corns to a fine paste.
4. Whisk Skimmed milk yogurt.
5. Dry roast bengal gram flour (*besan*) in a non-stick pan on low heat, stirring continuously until it gives a roasted aroma. Keep aside to cool.
6. Heat oil in a non-stick pan, add dried whole red chillies, cumin seeds and stir-fry briefly.
7. Add green chillies, coriander powder, turmeric powder, *besan* and stir well.
8. Add trimmed lady fingers, salt to taste and cook over medium heat, stirring frequently for five minutes.
9. Stir in the ginger and pepper corn paste. Reduce heat and add the whisked yogurt, mix well and cook covered for eight to ten minutes, stirring occasionally or until lady fingers are completely cooked.

### NUTRITIONAL INFORMATION

| Calories | Proteins | Fat | Carbohydrates | Fibre |
|---|---|---|---|---|
| 130 | 4.9 | 6.1 | 12.3 | 1.5 |

*Bhindi* or lady finger has high moisture content (90%) and low fat (0.2%) which makes it a low-calorie vegetable. It is also a good source of fibre and has a fair amount of folic acid and zinc. Seeds of lady fingers are a good source of protein.

# GAJAR

## *Dal Mel*

### INGREDIENTS

Split bengal gram (*Chana dal*) ........... ¾ cup
Carrots ........................... 3-4 medium sized
Onions ........................... 2 medium sized
Ginger ..................................... 1 inch knob
Garlic ......................................... 4-5 cloves
Tomatoes ......................... 2 medium sized
Fresh coriander leaves .................... ¼ cup
Oil ................................................ 1½ tspn
Bay leaf ................................................ 1
Cumin seeds .................................. 1 tspn
Red chilli powder ............................ 1 tspn
Coriander powder ......................... 1½ tspn
Turmeric powder ............................ ½ tspn
Salt ............................................. to taste

### METHOD OF PREPARATION

1. Pick, wash and soak *chana dal* for one to two hours in two cups of water. Drain and keep aside.
2. Peel, wash and cut carrots into one cm. cubes. Peel and chop onion, ginger and garlic. Wash tomatoes and finely chop. Clean fresh coriander leaves, wash thoroughly and then finely chop.
3. Heat oil in a non-stick pan, add bay leaf, cumin seeds and cook briefly. Add chopped onions and cook over medium heat till onion turns translucent. Add chopped ginger and garlic and stir-fry for half a minute.
4. Reduce the heat and add red chilli powder, coriander powder, turmeric powder and stir to mix well. Add chopped tomatoes and continue to cook for three to four minutes, stirring occasionally.
5. Drain and add the soaked *chana dal* and carrot cubes and mix well. Add one cup of water and salt to taste.
6. Cook on high heat till the water begins to boil, then lower the heat, cover and simmer till the *dal* is well cooked and the *masala* is almost dry. Adjust salt.
7. Garnish with chopped fresh coriander leaves and serve hot.

### NUTRITIONAL INFORMATION

| Calories | Proteins | Fat | Carbohydrates | Fibre |
|---|---|---|---|---|
| 105 | 2.8 | 4.6 | 14.0 | 1.1 |

Turmeric has very high amount of iron, magnesium and zinc. Medicinal properties of turmeric are world-renowned. It is commonly used in Ayurvedic medicines to purify blood, relieve pain, treatment of inflammation, either internal or external. Turmeric is also known to have antiseptic properties and is used extensively used in Indian households as a remedy to cuts and burns.

GOURMET

*Pasta*

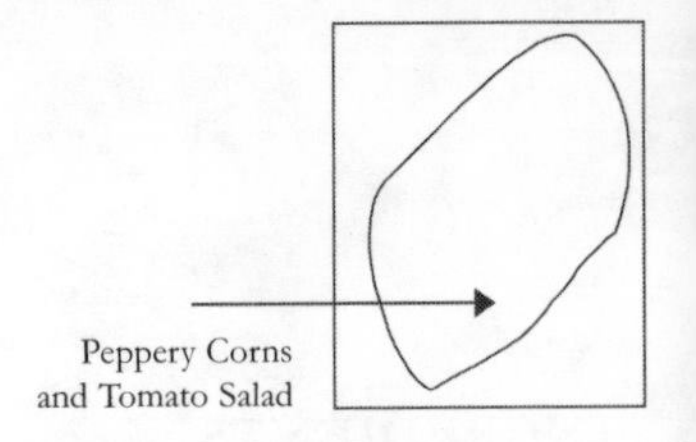
Peppery Corns and Tomato Salad

## INGREDIENTS

**For Pasta**

Whole wheat flour .......... 2 cups
Refined flour .......... ¾ cup
Salt .......... 1 tspn
Olive oil .......... 1 tspn
Eggs .......... 2

**For Sauce**

Tomatoes .......... 6 medium sized
Onion .......... 1 medium sized
Garlic .......... 3-4 cloves
Fresh basil .......... 5-6 leaves
Olive oil .......... 2 tspn
Red chilli flakes .......... 1 tspn
Crushed pepper corn .......... 1 tspn
Salt .......... to taste

## METHOD OF PREPARATION

**Chef's Tip:** *You can also make the pasta in the Pasta machine. The method of preparing the dough will remain the same.*

**Pasta**

1. Sieve both the flour together. Add salt, oil and mix in the eggs one by one. Sprinkle water and knead into a soft dough.
2. Rest the dough covered with a wet cloth for thirty minutes.
3. Knead the dough well once again. Sprinkle dry flour and roll the dough into as thin a sheet as possible. Trim the sides to a form a proper rectangle. Sprinkle dry flour liberally and using a rolling pin roll it up tightly.
4. With a sharp knife cut the roll in half to three fourth cm. thick sections. Open out the rolls and spread out on a mesh and let them dry in a cool airy place overnight.
5. Boil lots of water, add a little oil and salt. Add the pasta into the boiling water and stir. Cook till it is just done or '*al dente*'. Pour one cup cold water and drain the pasta well. Keep the pasta warm, while you prepare the sauce.

**Sauce**

1. Wash, remove the eye of the tomatoes and make a small incision at the bottom. Boil water and blanch the tomatoes for two minutes and remove immediately.
2. Peel, deseed and chop the tomatoes roughly.
3. Peel onion and garlic and finely chop. Wash and shred basil leaves.

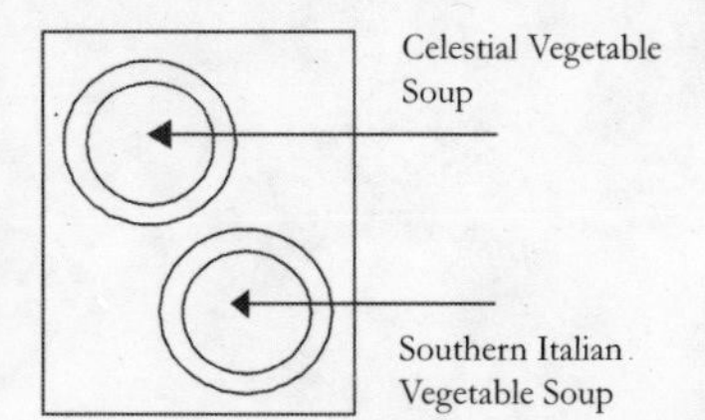


4. Heat olive oil in a non stick pan, add onion and garlic and sauté till they turn translucent. Add red chilli flakes and toss well. Add the fresh basil (Reserve some for garnishing).
5. Add the tomatoes and cook till it starts bubbling. Add the crushed pepper corn, salt and mix well.
6. Add cooked pasta to the sauce and toss over high heat till it is heated through. Adjust seasoning and serve hot garnished with shredded basil.

**NUTRITIONAL INFORMATION**

| Calories | Proteins | Fat | Carbohydrates | Fibre |
|---|---|---|---|---|
| 245 | 8.7 | 9.0 | 31.8 | 1.1 |

Olive oil is extracted from ripe olive fruits. This oil is nourishing and is a known laxative. When applied externally it treats skin infection. With alcohol it is a good hair tonic. It is used as a lubricant for muscular joints, and for chills, fever etc. Delicate babies absorb its nourishing properties well through the skin. It is well known for its protective role in heart disease

# MASALEDAAR TOFU

*Bhurji*

## INGREDIENTS

| | |
|---|---|
| Tofu (Beancurd) | 300 gms |
| Onions | 2 medium sized |
| Ginger | 1 inch knob |
| Tomatoes | 2 medium sized |
| Green chillies | 2 |
| Capsicum | 2 medium sized |
| Fresh coriander leaves | ¼ cup |
| Oil | 1 ½ tspns |
| Cumin seeds | 1 tspns |
| Turmeric powder | ½tspn |
| Cumin powder | 1 tspn |
| Coriander powder | 1 tblspn |
| Red chilli powder | 1 tspn |
| Salt | to taste |

## METHOD OF PREPARATION

1. Drain the tofu and crumble it into small pieces.
2. Peel and finely chop onion and ginger. Wash and finely chop tomatoes. Wash, remove stem, deseed and finely chop green chillies and capsicum. Wash and finely chop coriander leaves.
3. Heat oil in a non-stick pan, add cumin seeds and cook till they start to change colour. Add chopped onion, ginger and green chillies. Stir-fry till onion becomes translucent.
4. Dissolve turmeric powder, cumin powder, coriander powder and red chilli powder in half a cup of water and add this to the pan. Cook on medium heat for half a minute, stirring continuously.
5. Add chopped tomatoes and cook on high heat for two minutes, stirring continuously. Stir in crumbled tofu, chopped capsicum and salt to taste. Mix well.
6. Reduce heat and cook for two to three minutes, tossing frequently to prevent sticking, the natural inclination of tofu.
7. Sprinkle chopped coriander leaves on top and serve.

## NUTRITIONAL INFORMATION

| Calories | Proteins | Fat | Carbohydrates | Fibre |
|---|---|---|---|---|
| 180 | 20.7 | 4.5 | 1.0 | 0.6 |

Soyabean curd or Tofu has a bland taste and has cheese-like appearance. It is commonly used in Oriental cooking. Tofu is rich in protien, polyunsaturated fats, B comples Vitamins and iron. Paneer can easily be substituted with tofu.

# *Arhar Dal*

## INGREDIENTS

*Arhar dal* ........ ¾ cup
Cauliflower ........ ¼ medium sized
Carrot ........ 1 medium sized
French beans ........ 6-8
Drumsticks ........ 2
Green chillies ........ 1-2
Ginger ........ 1 inch knob
Garlic ........ 4-5 cloves
Turmeric powder ........ ½ tspn
Oil ........ 1½ tspn
Cumin seeds ........ 1 tspn
Red chilli powder ........ ½ tblspn
Coriander powder ........ 1 tblspn
Tamarind pulp ........ 1 tblspn
Salt ........ to taste

## METHOD OF PREPARATION

1. Pick *dal*, wash twice or thrice times with plenty of water. Soak in sufficient water.
2. Trim and cut cauliflower into small florets, wash and soak in warm salted water. Peel, wash and cut carrot into one inch dices. String French beans and cut into one inch dices.
3. Wash and cut the drumsticks into two inch pieces. Wash, remove stem and slit green chillies into two. Peel, wash and chop ginger and garlic.
4. Drain the *dal* and cook in three and a half cups of water with slit green chillies and turmeric powder in a pressure cooker for four to five minutes or until soft.
5. Similarly cook the cauliflower, carrots, drumstick and French beans in one cup water in the pressure cooker for three to four minutes or until tender.
6. Heat oil in a non-stick pan, add cumin seeds, stir briefly and add chopped ginger, garlic and sauté for a while.
7. Add red chilli powder and coriander powder and stir briefly. Dilute the tamarind pulp in quarter cup water and stir into the pan.
8. Add cooked lentils and vegetables along with its cooking liquor to the pan, mix well and add salt.
9. Continue to cook for three to four minutes on medium heat or till all the ingredients combine well and it starts bubbling. Serve hot with steamed unpolished rice.

### NUTRITIONAL INFORMATION

| Calories | Proteins | Fat | Carbohydrates | Fibre |
|---|---|---|---|---|
| 125 | 7.1 | 2.3 | 18.6 | 2.2 |

*Arhar dal* (*Toor dal*) or Pigeon Pea is one of the most common *dals* used in Indian kitchens. It is high in protein (22%) and low in fat (1.7%). *Arhar dal* is high in phosphorous, potassium, copper, magnesium and selenium. The fresh beans of *Arhar*, which are used as vegetable, have high fibre content (6%). It is a good idea to add vegetables to *dal* preparations to increase vegetable consumption.

# METHI TOMATO

## *Paneer*

### INGREDIENTS

| | |
|---|---|
| Low fat paneer | 200 gms |
| Fresh *methi* | 1 medium sized bunch |
| Tomatoes | 4 medium sized |
| Ginger | 1 inch knob |
| Garlic | 6 cloves |
| Onions | 2 medium sized |
| Green chillies | 2-3 |
| Oil | 1 tblspn |
| Kashmiri red chilli powder | 1 tspn |
| Coriander powder | 1 tblspn |
| Salt | to taste |
| Dried mango powder (*Amchur*) | 1 tspn |

### METHOD OF PREPARATION

1. Cut paneer into half inch sized cubes.
2. Clean, wash and chop fresh *methi* leaves.
3. Wash and finely chop the tomatoes. Peel ginger, garlic and onions. Finely chop the onions.
4. Wash green chillies, remove stem and grind to a paste with the ginger and garlic.
5. Heat oil in a non-stick pan, add the chopped onion and sauté for three to four minutes or till it just starts turning brown.
6. Add ginger, garlic and green chilli paste, stir-fry briefly and add kashmiri red chilli powder, coriander powder and salt to taste. Mix well.
7. Immediately, add the chopped *methi* leaves and cook on medium heat, stirring frequently for six to eight minutes, stirring continuously or until the *methi* leaves are completely cooked and dry.
8. Add the chopped tomatoes, stir and cook over high heat for two to three minutes. Add half cup water, cover and simmer for three to four minutes.
9. Add the paneer pieces, sprinkle dried mango powder and mix well.
10. Cook to heat through and serve immediately.

### NUTRITIONAL INFORMATION

| Calories | Proteins | Fat | Carbohydrates | Fibre |
|---|---|---|---|---|
| 230 | 11.2 | 12 | 17.5 | 1.1 |

Calcium is required for the formation and maintenance of skeleton and bones. It is required for normal muscle contraction to make limbs move, contraction of heart, nerve activity and blood clotting. In this recipe apart from paneer, *methi* leaves are also high in calcium. It is interesting to know that body can utilize calcium eaten in the form of betel leaves (*paan*) with slaked lime (calcium hydroxide) or *chuna*, which is a practice quite common in India. However the *paan* needs to be chewed and eaten quickly and without tobacco, which is an irritant to the mouth.

# SPROUTED HARACHANA

## *Amti*

### INGREDIENTS

| | | | |
|---|---|---|---|
| Green *Chana* | 1 cup | Mustard seeds | ¼ tspn |
| Garlic | 3-4 cloves | Dried whole red chillies | 2 |
| Green Chillies | 2-3 | Tamarind pulp | 2 tblspn |
| *Ajwain* | ¼ tspn | Turmeric powder | ½ tspn |
| Oil | 1 ½ tspn | Salt | to taste |
| Asafoetida | ¼ tspn | Jaggery | 1 tspn |

### METHOD OF PREPARATION

1. Wash the *chana* two to three times and soak in plenty of water for four to five hours. Drain, tie in a moist cloth and keep in a warm place for two days or until they sprout. Ensure that the cloth is always moist.
2. Peel and finely chop garlic. Wash, remove stem and finely chop the green chillies. Crush the *ajwain* lightly and keep.
3. Heat oil in a non-stick pan, add asafoetida powder and mustard seeds and let them crackle. Break the dried red chillies into two and add to the pan.
4. Add chopped garlic and chopped green chillies and stir-fry for half a minute.
5. Dilute the tamarind with half cup water and add to the pan.
6. Sprinkle turmeric powder, salt, jaggery and stir well over high heat and cook till the jaggery dissolves.
7. Add the sprouted green *chana* and the crushed *ajwain*.
8. Toss well to mix thoroughly, remove immediately from heat and serve hot.

### NUTRITIONAL INFORMATION

| Calories | Proteins | Fat | Carbohydrates | Fibre |
|---|---|---|---|---|
| 120 | 3.0 | 4.8 | 16.2 | 0.8 |

Sprouting or germination of cereals and legumes helps its digestibility. Sprouting increases Vitamins and reduces bulk on cooking. It also decreases phytate (anti-nutrient) level. Digestibility increases due to production of amylase (an enzyme which helps digestion of carbohydrate). As such pulses or cereals do not have any Vitamin A or Vitamin C, but germination increases the Vitamin C content.

# SHANGHAI STIR FRIED

## *Vegetables*

### INGREDIENTS

Carrot ........ 1 medium sized
Capsicum ........ 1 medium sized
Onion ........ 1 medium sized
Cauliflower ........ ¼ small sized
Tender Baby corns ........ 6-8
Chinese cabbage ........ ½ medium sized
Fresh mushrooms ........ 8-10
Spring onions ........ 2
Garlic ........ 6-8 cloves
Water chest nut(optional) ........ 3-4
Cornflour ........ 1 tblspn
Oil ........ 1 tspn
Light soya sauce ........ 1 tblspn
Salt ........ to taste
White pepper powder ........ 4 tspn

### METHOD OF PREPARATION

**Chef's Tip:**

*In India, cornstarch is commonly referred to as cornflour. For ease of readers we have also used the term cornflour.*

1. Peel carrot, wash and cut lengthwise and thinly slice.
2. Wash capsicum, halve, deseed and then cut into one inch sized pieces.
3. Peel and cut onion into quarters and separate onion segments.
4. Wash and separate cauliflower into small sized florets and slice them into two through the stem.
5. Trim and slice the baby corns into three to four pieces diagonally. Separate Chinese cabbage leaves and wash thoroughly under running water. Drain well and cut into one inch sized pieces.
6. Wash mushrooms thoroughly and cut them into quarters. Peel, wash and slice spring onions along with some greens. Peel garlic and crush lightly. Peel and slice water chest nut.
7. Dissolve cornflour in half a cup of water. Keep aside.
8. Heat oil in a non-stick wok, add crushed garlic, stir and add carrot, cauliflower, baby corn and mushroom. Toss well and sprinkle a little water on vegetables. Cook on high heat, stirring frequently, for two to three minutes.
9. Add onion segments, capsicum, water chest nut and Chinese cabbage. Stir-fry on high flame again for two minutes, stirring frequently. Add soya sauce, white pepper powder and salt to taste, toss well.
10. Mix cornflour dissolved in water and add to the vegetables, stirring continuously. Cook further for a minute. Serve immediately.

### NUTRITIONAL INFORMATION

| Calories | Proteins | Fat | Carbohydrates | Fibre |
|---|---|---|---|---|
| 135 | 3.4 | 8.6 | 12.9 | 1.6 |

Stalks of spring onion can make an excellent alternative to more commonly used green leafy vegetables. Like all other green leafy vegetables it is nutrient dense and contains nutrients like calcium, iron, B-carotene and Vitamin C (in uncooked form).

# THAI VEGETABLE
## *in Red Curry*

**INGREDIENTS**

Carrots ........................................ 4 medium
Capsicum ........................................ 1 medium
Cauliflower ........................................ ½ small
Cabbage ........................................ ½ small
French beans ........................................ 100 gms
Roasted peanuts ........................................ 4 tblspns
Oil ........................................ 1 tblspn
Lemon juice ........................................ 1 tspn
Salt ........................................ to taste
Thin coconut milk ........................................ ¾ cup
Bean sprout ........................................ 100 gms

**For Red Curry Paste**

Dried whole red chillies ........................................ 8
Lemon grass stalk ........................................ 4 inch
Coriander seeds ........................................ 4 tspns
Cumin seeds ........................................ 2 tspn
Pepper corns ........................................ 6
Onion, peeled and sliced ........................................ 2 medium
Garlic ........................................ 4 cloves
Salt ........................................ to taste

**METHOD OF PREPARATION**

1. Wash and peel carrots and cut into 1 x 3 cm. long sticks.
2. Wash capsicum, halve, deseed and cut into 1 x 3 cm. long pieces.
3. Wash and cut cauliflower into small florets. Wash and cut cabbage into one cm. sized pieces. Wash and string french beans and then cut them into three cms. long pieces.
4. Crush roasted peanuts coarsely.
5. To make red curry paste, mix dried whole red chillies, lemon grass, coriander seeds, cumin seeds, pepper corns, chopped onion, garlic, salt and a little water, then grind into a fine paste.
6. Heat oil in a non-stick pan, add carrots, cauliflower, french beans and half a cup of water. Let it cook on medium heat for five to six minutes, stirring occasionally. Add cabbage and capsicum, mix well. Add red curry paste, stir well, cook on high heat for one or two minutes.
7. Stir in a lemon juice and salt. Mix well and add thin coconut milk. Simmer for two minutes and stir in bean sprouts and crushed roasted peanuts.

**NUTRITIONAL INFORMATION**

| Calories | Proteins | Fat | Carbohydrates | Fibre |
|---|---|---|---|---|
| 280 | 9.5 | 14.3 | 29.7 | 3.9 |

This dish supplies good amount of fibre from vegetables and sprouts. Note that the carrots used are not peeled, which increases the fibre content. Fibre is the indigestible portion of the stems, roots, skin and leaves of plant food. People who eat more fibres have lowered risk of developing many kinds of cancer, heart diseases, intestinal diseases and diabetes. Fibre helps to keep the digestive tract healthy, prevent constipation and lower cholesterol. One of the benefits of eating high fibre foods is that they tend to be low fat foods as well. Fibre can add bulk to the diet without adding calories.

# MUSHROOM SOYAWADI

## *Masala*

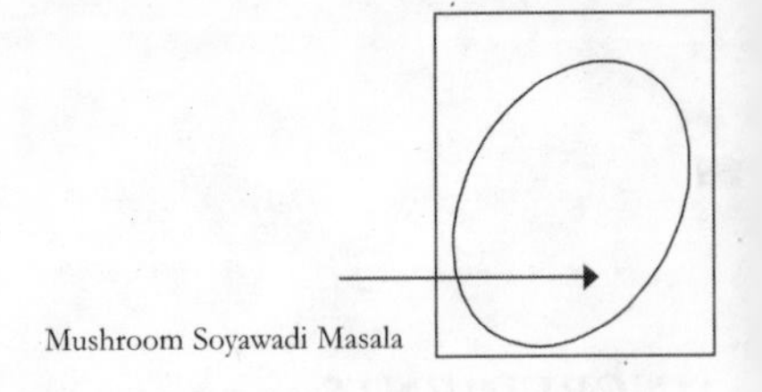

Mushroom Soyawadi Masala

### INGREDIENTS

| | | | |
|---|---|---|---|
| Fresh mushrooms | 15-20 | Bay leaf | 1 |
| Soya bean *wadi* | 1½ cup | Crushed pepper corn | ½ tspn |
| Ginger | 1 inch knob | Red chilli powder | 1 tspn |
| Garlic | 5 cloves | Coriander powder | 1 tspn |
| Onions | 3 medium sized | Turmeric powder | ¼ tspn |
| Tomatoes | 2 medium sized | *Garam masala* powder | ½ tspn |
| Mint | a few sprigs | Salt | to taste |
| Oil | 1½ tspn | | |

### METHOD OF PREPARATION

1. Wash mushrooms in flowing water, drain well and cut into quarters.
2. Soak soya bean *wadi* in warm water for fifteen to twenty minutes. Squeeze to remove excess water, cut them into two and keep aside.
3. Peel, wash and chop ginger, garlic and onion.
4. Wash tomatoes and finely chop. Clean mint, wash thoroughly in plenty of water and finely chop.
5. Heat oil in a non-stick pan, add bay leaf, crushed pepper corn and stir-fry briefly.
6. Add chopped ginger, garlic and cook on high flame for half a minute, stirring continuously.
7. Add chopped onion and continue cooking until onion turns translucent.
8. Add red chilli powder, coriander powder and turmeric powder and stir well. Mix in the chopped tomatoes, add salt and continue cooking over medium heat.
9. Add the mushrooms and soaked soya bean *wadi.* Stir well.
10. Sprinkle *garam masala* powder, chopped mint and salt. Mix well. Cook over high heat for two minutes. Cover and simmer over medium heat for two to three minutes.

### NUTRITIONAL INFORMATION

| Calories | Proteins | Fat | Carbohydrates | Fibre |
|---|---|---|---|---|
| 150 | 14.7 | 4.4 | 3.0 | 0.4 |

Soya bean contains three major macro nutrients — protein, carbohydrate and fat. Soya beans are the only vegetable that contain complete protein. The protein quality is virtually equivalent to that of meat, milk and egg protein. Almost 40% of calories from soya bean are derived from protein, making soya bean higher in protein than any other legumes and many animal products. Unlike many other good sources of protein, soya beans are low in saturated fat and are cholesterol free. Many studies show that soya foods are helpful in fighting many types of cancer. Moreover for the past thirty years investigations have shown that consumption of soya protein selectively decreases total and LDL (bad) cholesterol and maintains HDL (good) cholesterol.

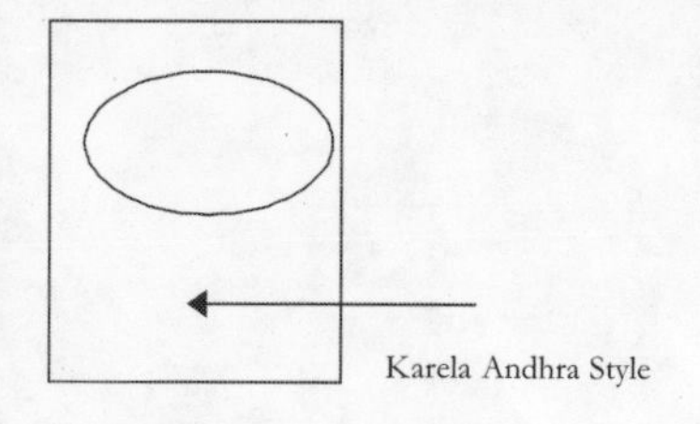

Karela Andhra Style

# KARELA
## *Andhra Style*

### INGREDIENTS

Bitter gourd (*Karela*) ... 4-5 medium sized
Salt .................. to taste
Onions .................. 2 medium sized
Ginger .................. 1 inch knob
Garlic .................. 5 cloves
Dried whole red chillies .................. 4
Coriander seeds .................. 1 tblspns
Cumin seeds .................. 1 tspn
White sesame seeds .................. 1 tspn
Oil .................. 1½ tspn
Tomato puree .................. ¼ cup
Grated jaggery .................. 2 tblspns
Tamarind pulp .................. 2 tblspns

### METHOD OF PREPARATION

1. Wash, scrape and cut *karela* in half, length wise; remove seeds and thinly slice. Apply salt and leave aside for ten to fifteen minutes. Wash with plenty of water, drain and squeeze out excess water.
2. Peel and chop onions. Peel ginger and wash well. Peel garlic. Grind ginger and garlic to a fine paste.
3. Roast whole red chillies, coriander seeds, cumin seeds and white sesame seeds on a medium hot *tawa* till light brown, stirring continuously. Cool the mixture and then grind to a fine powder.
4. Heat oil in a non-stick pan and add sliced *karela* and stir-fry for four to five minutes or till slightly browned. Add chopped onions and stir-fry for three to four minutes.
5. Add ginger and garlic paste and again stir-fry for one to two minutes.
6. Add tomato puree and cook further for a few minutes.
7. Add ground powder, grated jaggery, tamarind pulp and salt.
8. Stir well and add one cup of water and bring to a boil.
9. Reduce to medium heat, cover and simmer for five minute.

### NUTRITIONAL INFORMATION

| Calories | Proteins | Fat | Carbohydrates | Fibre |
|---|---|---|---|---|
| 130 | 2.6 | 9.7 | 11.0 | 1.7 |

*Karela* or bitter gourd is a low calorie vegetable. It has fair amount of B-carotene, Vitamin C and minerals like zinc. Over the years bitter gourd has been extensively studied, especially for its anti-diabetic property. Majority of work has documented its beneficial effect. The possible effect is that it stimulates enzymes, which mediate insulin secretion in control of diabetes.

# RATATOUILLE

## INGREDIENTS

Long eggplants (Brinjal) ..... 2 medium sized
Zucchini .......................... 2 medium sized
Salt.............................................. to taste
Onion............................... 2 medium sized
Garlic ........................................ 4 cloves
Tomatoes .......................... 3 medium sized
Capsicum.......................... 2 medium sized
Olive oil ........................................ 1 tblspn
Tomato puree ............................. 4 tblspns
Coriander powder ......................... ¼ tspn
Cinnamon powder ......................... a pinch
Basil leaves ...................................... a few
White pepper powder ................... to taste

## METHOD OF PREPARATION

1. Wash and half eggplants and zucchini lengthways. Cut them further into thick slices.
2. Place eggplants in a colander and sprinkle with salt. Top with a heavy plate and leave to degorge for one hour.
3. Peel and slice the onions into rings. Peel and chop the garlic.
4. Wash and remove eye of the tomatoes, make a cross slit on the bottom side and immerse in boiling water for half a minute.
5. Drain the tomatoes, peel, deseed and chop them roughly.
6. Cut the capsicum into halves, deseed and cut into thin strips.
7. Heat the olive oil in a non-stick pan and cook onion over low heat until translucent. Stir in the tomato puree and cook on medium heat for three to four minutes, stirring occasionally.
8. Rinse sliced eggplant and drain well. Add drained eggplant and sliced zucchini to the cooking pan.
9. Add the garlic and capsicum and simmer for about five minutes.
10. Add the blanched and chopped tomatoes, shredded basil, salt and pepper. Stir once or twice and cook over medium heat for about ten minutes, stirring frequently.
11. Adjust the seasoning and serve hot.

### NUTRITIONAL INFORMATION

| Calories | Proteins | Fat | Carbohydrates | Fibre |
|---|---|---|---|---|
| 135 | 6.6 | 4. 9 | 20.5 | 3.3 |

Tomatoes are a good source of B-carotene, Vitamin C and lycopene. Lycopene is also a carotenoid. However studies have shown that lycopene is twice as powerful as B-carotene in its role of anti-oxidant. Tomatoes, tomato products, guava, grapefruit, papaya and watermelon are all good sources of lycopene.

# BEANS WITH TOMATO

## *Yogurt Sauce*

**INGREDIENTS**

French beans .................................... 20-25
Spring onions ................. 3 medium sized
Ginger............................ 1 one inch knob
Garlic ......................................... 5 cloves
Dried whole red chillies ......................... 2
Skimmed milk yogurt .................. 1½ cup
Maize flour .................................. 1 tblspn
Tomatoes ......................... 3 medium sized
Oil ............................................... 2 tspns
Salt........................................... to taste

**METHOD OF PREPARATION**

1. String French beans, wash them and then cut into three inch long pieces. Blanch in salted boiling water until cooked. Strain, (reserve the water to use as stock) refresh in cold water and then drain.
2. Slit the cooked beans into two and tie them up in bundles with spring onion stalk.
3. Wash, trim and finely chop spring onion. Peel and wash ginger and garlic. Grind ginger and garlic to a fine paste. Crush dry whole red chillies.
4. Beat Skimmed milk yogurt with maize flour.
5. Wash tomatoes, make a cross with knife and then blanch in boiling water for thirty seconds. Remove peel, deseed and then chop.
6. Heat the oil in a non-stick pan, add chopped spring onion and cook until it turns translucent.
7. Add the paste of ginger and garlic. Stir for a moment.
8. Add tomatoes and cook further for two to three minutes.
9. Reduce the heat and add beaten skimmed milk yogurt and maize flour mixture, mix well, add salt to taste, and stir continuously.
10. Warm the cooked bean bundles just before serving, in a microwave for one minute on HIGH or by briefly dipping them in boiling hot water or stock. Top with the prepared yogurt sauce.
11. Sprinkle the crushed chillies and serve hot.

**Chef's Tip:**

*To preserve natural colour of green vegetables, cook them uncovered and do not overcook green vegetables, and do not add any baking soda.*

**NUTRITIONAL INFORMATION**

| Calories | Proteins | Fat | Carbohydrates | Fibre |
|---|---|---|---|---|
| 115 | 5.9 | 2.2 | 16.7 | 4.3 |

Selenium, currently in news for its antioxidant properties, is also required for normal thyroid functioning. It provides immunity and prevents male infertility. But a word of caution, selenium must not be taken in excessive quantities in the form of tablets. It is naturally present in food items like onions and yogurt.

# SWEET CORN
## *Kadhi*

### INGREDIENTS

| | |
|---|---|
| Green chillies | 2-3 |
| Ginger | 1-inch knob |
| Onions | 2 medium sized |
| Skimmed milk yogurt | 1 cup |
| Bengal gram flour (*Besan*) | 2 tblspns |
| Turmeric powder | 1 tspn |
| Sweet corn kernels (Frozen or Tinned) | ½ cup |
| Sweet corn, cream style | ¼ cup |
| Salt | to taste |
| Oil | 1½ tspn |
| Mustard seeds | ¼ tspn |
| Fennel seeds | ½ tspn |
| *Kalonji* | ¼ tspn |
| Dried whole red chillies | 4 |

### METHOD OF PREPARATION

**Chef's Tip:** *While using dry or fresh corn kernels, cook in salted water till tender before adding to the kadhi.*

1. Wash green chillies, remove stem and roughly chop.
2. Peel, wash and grind ginger to a fine paste along with the chopped green chillies. Peel and slice onion.
3. Whisk the skimmed milk yogurt with the bengal gram flour and turmeric, thoroughly. Stir in two cups of water and mix.
4. Pour the yogurt mixture into a thick-bottomed pan and bring it to a boil. Reduce the heat and gradually mix in the ginger and green chilli paste, sliced onion and sweet corn, cream style. Stir well and cook for two to three minutes.
5. Add the sweet corn kernels and salt to the cooking *kadhi* and pour one cup water.
6. Simmer over medium heat for eight to ten minutes, stirring frequently or till it thickens to a curry consistency.
7. Heat oil in a small tempering pan, add mustard seeds, fennel seeds, *kalonji* and dry whole red chillies broken into two. Stir continuously and cook till they start crackling.
8. Pour this over the sweet corn *kadhi* and immediately cover with a lid to trap all the flavours and aroma.
9. Stir well. Serve hot with steamed unpolished rice.

### NUTRITIONAL INFORMATION

| Calories | Proteins | Fat | Carbohydrates | Fibre |
|---|---|---|---|---|
| 95 | 3.9 | 2.4 | 13.5 | 0.5 |

Fennel seeds are similar to anise seeds. They are known to aid digestion. One litre of water boiled with 2 teaspoons of fennel seeds for fifteen to twenty minutes, and strained is commonly used for infants and children.

# QUICK PRESSURE COOKED
## *Vegetables*

**INGREDIENTS**

Carrots ........................ 2 medium sized
Ash Gourd (*Lauki*) ............ ½ small sized
Cauliflower ..................... ½ small sized
Cabbage ......................... ¼ small sized
Potato ........................... 1 medium sized
French beans .......................... 10-12
Tomato .......................... 1 medium sized
Capsicum ...................... 1 medium sized
Oil ............................................... 1 tspn
Bay leaf ............................................ 1
Crushed pepper corn ..................... 1 tspn
Roasted cumin powder ................. ½ tspn
Salt ........................................ to taste

**METHOD OF PREPARATION**

1. Wash, peel and cut carrots into one and a half cm. sized pieces. Wash, peel and cut *lauki* into one and a half cm. sized pieces. Wash and separate cauliflower into small florets. Wash and cut cabbage into one and a half cm. sized pieces.
2. Wash, peel and cut potato into one and a half cm. pieces and keep them soaked in water. Wash, string and cut french beans into one and a half cm. pieces. Wash and cut tomato into eight pieces. Wash, halve, deseed and cut capsicum into one and a half cm. sized pieces.
3. Heat oil in a pressure cooker, add bay leaf and crushed pepper corn, stir-fry briefly. Add vegetables, roasted cumin powder, salt, and mix well. Stir-fry for two to three minutes.
4. Cover and cook under pressure for five to six minutes. Remove from heat.
5. Serve immediately.

**NUTRITIONAL INFORMATION**

| Calories | Proteins | Fat | Carbohydrates | Fibre |
|---|---|---|---|---|
| 100 | 2.3 | 4.3 | 15.4 | 1.9 |

Pressure cooking not only saves time and fuel, but also retains more nutrients and flavour if cooked rightly and for the right time. Pressure cooking can greatly shorten the cooking time. Shorter the cooking time, less the destruction of Vitamins will be. Pressure cooking can be one of the healthy alternatives for people who like to cook with minimum oil.

# Corn Pie

## INGREDIENTS

Onions .......... 2 medium sized
Garlic .......... 3 cloves
Capsicum .......... 2 medium sized
Carrot .......... 1 medium sized
Tomatoes .......... 2 mesium sized
Kidney beans (*Rajma*) .......... 2 cups
Red chilli powder .......... 2 tspns
Cumin powder .......... 1 tspn
Oil .......... 2 tspns
White wine (optional) .......... 2 tblspns

**For Pie Crust**

Maize flour .......... 2 cups
Whole wheat flour .......... ½ cup
Baking powder .......... 2 tspns
Salt .......... 1 tspn
Water .......... ½ cup
Oil .......... to grease baking dish

## METHOD OF PREPARATION

1. Peel and finely chop onions and garlic.
2. Wash capsicum, halve, deseed and finely chop. Wash and peel carrot. Cut it into one fourth inch sized pieces. Wash and puree tomatoes in a blender, keep aside.
3. Pick kidney beans, wash well and then soak for six to eight hours. Boil in sufficient salted water until soft. Drain and leave aside.
4. Preheat oven to 200 degrees Celsius. Mix all the pie ingredients and knead well until smooth.
5. Grease a 9 x 12 inch baking dish. Pat half the dough into the bottom of the dish.
6. Spread a long sheet of butter paper and pat remaining dough on to it, roughly in the shape of 9 x 12 inch rectangle.
7. Heal oil in a non-stick pan, add chopped onion and cook until soft and translucent.
8. Add chopped garlic, capsicum, diced carrots and cook for five minutes.
9. Add boiled kidney beans, pureed tomatoes, red chilli powder, cumin powder and white wine. Cook covered on reduced flame until vegetables are tender.
10. Put the filling into prepared baking dish, lay the remaining rolled pie dough onto it, press the edges to seal.
11. Bake for thirty five to forty minutes or until brown.

## NUTRITIONAL INFORMATION

| Calories | Proteins | Fat | Carbohydrates | Fibre |
|---|---|---|---|---|
| 225 | 7.5 | 8.4 | 41.7 | 2.2 |

Corn that has been dried and ground in to a meal or flour is included in the grain group, whereas fresh , frozen and canned corn is usually classified as a vegetable. The yellow variety has more B-carotene than the white variety. Coarse whole maize flour also has a good amount of fiber.

# SEAFOOD

Fish enjoys a unique status as it is obtained from water unlike other foods, which are available on land. People living near the sea or on banks of rivers are more likely to be fish eaters. In many parts of the world, fish is eaten as a staple food.

Fish can be divided into two classes, lean and fat. Lean or white fish contains less than 2% of fat and 20% of protein with energy values ranging from 50-80 kcals/100 gms. The composition of all non-fatty fish is similar. They are light and easily digestible. Fatty fish contain 10-24% protein, 5-15% fat and so have a higher energy value earning form 80-160 kcls/100 gms. They are high in Vitamin D as compared to white fish. Oily fish are salmon, anchovie, herring, eel, white bast, sardines and sprates. Intermediate species of fish, which contain 2-7% fat are hake, halibut, mackerel, mullet and trout.

The fat soluble Vitamin A and D are found concentrated in the oils of big fish. The only rich sources of Vitamin D are the liver oils of fish. Oils extracted from the livers of shark, cod and halibut are very rich in these Vitamins. These fatty fish obtain Vitamin A by ingesting plankton living near the surface of the sea, and get exposed to sunlight. The green plants (plankton) are rich in carotenes (pro-Vitamin A). Thus they become a store house of Vitamin A and D. They are also rich in Vitamin E as compared to other oils.Vitamin B complex, especially niacin is present in good amount. Though a good amount of Vitamin C is present in raw fish, it is destroyed on cooking.

Marine fish and shell fish are a richer source of iodine than fresh water fish. If sea fish is eaten twice a week it will supply enough iodine to prevent goitre in normal circumstances. Sea fish are also rich in fluoride. Small fish as sprats and sardines can be useful source of calcium when eaten whole, together with bones and may supply up to 400 mg. of calcium/100 gms. Fish also contains fair amount of copper.

Shell fish, lobster, cray fish, crabs, shrimps and prawns are common salt water shell fish and they have very little fat and a calorie value of about 50 cals/100 gms. They are a rich source of protein (15%) and minerals, particularly iodine. Oysters are the richest food source of zinc and contain upto 100 mg/100 gms.

Fish contains small amount of connective tissues and take very little time to cook. The best way of cooking fish is by steaming, to preserve its nutrients. Maximum loss occurs when fish is boiled and the water is thrown away. Cooking with vinegar increases the availability of calcium as the bones become soft and can be eaten. Fried fish has a high calorific value due to the retention of fat. Fish is a rich source of omega 3 fatty acids, which have many health benefits. These fatty acids lower the incidence of atherosclerosis commonly referred to as clogged arteries. Consumption of 100-200 gms. of fish, twice a week may reduce the risk of coronary heart diseases and provide protection against cancer.

However, one must note that consumption of shell fish is the commonest cause of allergies. Shell fish which is not stored or cooked properly, may precipitate stomach upset and diarrhoea. Shell fish consume plankton which sometimes contain the toxin called 'saxitoxin' which remains in the tissue of the shell fish and is not destroyed on cooking. Fish is more or less acid forming, hence a fish diet should be supplemented, with good amount of vegetables and fruits, which are alkaline.

In short, fish eaters have a lot to cheer about since it is a rich source of several nutrients. Fish is regarded as one of the finest dietary items available to us.

# CREOLE
## *King Fish*

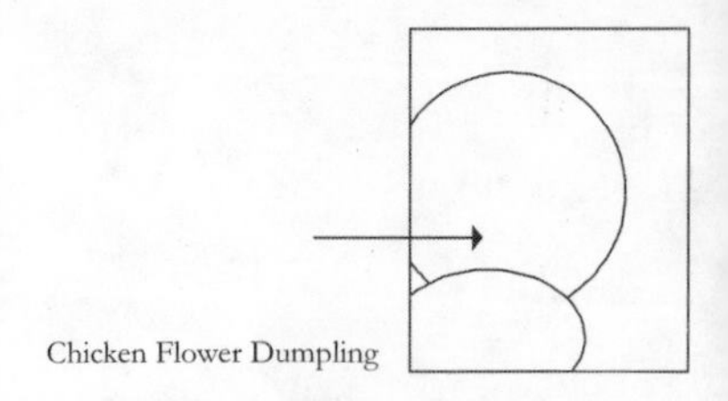
Chicken Flower Dumpling

### INGREDIENTS

Tomatoes ........................ 4 medium sized
Garlic ........................................ 6-8 cloves
Onion ............................. 1 medium sized
Green chilli ............................................ 1
Fresh coriander leaves .................... ¼ cup
King fish .............. 4 one inch thick slices
Lemon juice ................................ 2 tblspns
Dried oregano leaves ..................... ½ tspn
Dried basil leaves ........................... ¼ tspn
Dried thyme leaves .......................... ¼ tspn
Tobasco sauce ................................. 1 tspn
Salt ................................................. to taste
Oil ...................................................... 1 tspn

### METHOD OF PREPARATION

1. Wash and roughly chop two tomatoes and puree the rest in blender. Process until nearly smooth. Set aside.
2. Peel and finely chop garlic. Peel and slice the onion. Wash, remove stem and break the chilli into two. Wash and roughly chop fresh coriander leaves.
3. Wash fish slices and pat dry with a clean and absorbent kitchen cloth. Apply lemon juice and keep for five to ten minutes.
4. Cook chopped tomatoes, pureed tomatoes, sliced onion, chopped garlic, green chilli and one cup water in a non-stick sauce pan over medium heat for five to seven minutes, stirring frequently.
5. Reduce heat and stir in dried herbs, Tobasco sauce and salt. Cook for three to four minutes, or until liquid is reduced and sauce thickens, stirring frequently. Remove from heat and stir in chopped coriander leaves. Cover to keep warm.
6. Heat a non-stick pan, brush it with oil and place King fish slices. Cook on medium heat, turning once, for four to six minutes, or until fish is firm and opaque and just begins to flake.
7. Serve each fish slice topped with about three tablespoons of the prepared Creole style sauce.

### NUTRITIONAL INFORMATION

| Calories | Proteins | Fat | Carbohydrates | Fibre |
|---|---|---|---|---|
| 95 | 6.8 | 1.3 | 6.6 | 0.8 |

Tobasco is very high in sodium content and hence should not be used for those with salt restricted diet. Even in normal use it should be used in extremely limited amount.

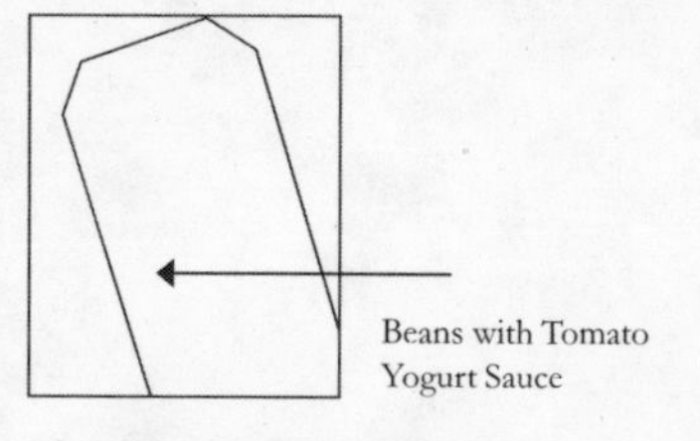


# DIJON STYLE

## *Fish*

### INGREDIENTS

Boneless fish .................................. 4 fillets
Salt .............................................. to taste
Mustard powder,
preferably Dijon ........................... 1 tblspn
Lemon juice .................................. 1 tblspn
Cornflour .................................. 1½ tblspn
Onion .............................. 2 medium sized
Garlic ............................................ 5 cloves
Fresh parsley ......................... a few sprigs
Oil ................................................ 1 tblspns
Worcestershire sauce .................... 1 tblspn
Fish stock or Water ...................... 1½ cups
Bay leaves ............................................... 2
White wine (optional) ..................... ½ cup
Pepper corns ........................................ 8-10

### METHOD OF PREPARATION

1. Clean, trim and wash fish fillets. Marinate the fish fillets in salt, mustard powder and lemon juice. Dissolve the cornflour in quarter cup water and keep.
2. Peel and slice onion. Peel, crush and chop garlic. Wash, trim stem and finely chop the fresh parsley.
3. Heat oil in a non stick pan and sauté the sliced onion till it turns translucent and mix in Worcestershire sauce. Cook on medium heat, stirring occasionally for a minute more and remove from heat.
4. Spread the cooked onion evenly in the serving dish or plate and keep warm.
5. Boil the fish stock or water in a shallow pan. Add bay leaves, white wine, chopped garlic, crushed pepper corn and salt.
6. Reduce the heat and slide in the fish fillet and poach at simmering point for three to four minutes or until the fish is just cooked. Gently lift the cooked fish fillets with a slotted spoon, drain well, place over the cooked onion in the serving dish or plate, and keep warm.
7. Reheat the cooking liquor and gradually mix in the dissolved cornflour, stirring continuously till it thickens to sauce consistency. Adjust seasoning.
8. Remove the bay leaf and pour over the cooked fish fillet to evenly coat.
9. Garnish liberally with chopped parsley and serve hot immediately.

### NUTRITIONAL INFORMATION

| Calories | Proteins | Fat | Carbohydrates | Fibre |
|---|---|---|---|---|
| 195 | 13. 8 | 4.4 | 9. 1 | 0. 4 |

Oils are fats that are liquid at room temperature. One gram of any oil gives 9 calories or 1 tablespoon gives about 45-50 calories. Oil as such contains no cholesterol. Oils are made of polyunsaturated fats, which supply essential fatty acids (EFA). These fatty acids are not made in the body and have to supplied via food. EFA have important role in fat metabolism. EFA deficiency in infants causes poor growth and lowered resistance to infections. Oils when exposed to warm, moist air turn rancid and produce toxins.

# LEMON STEAMED

## *Fish*

### INGREDIENTS

Boneless fish .......................... 4 thick slices
Lemon juice .................................. 3 tblspns
Salt .................................................. to taste
Ginger ..................................... 1 inch knob
Garlic ............................................ 4 cloves
Spring onions ............................................ 2
Celery ................................ ½ medium stalk
Lemon ....................................................... 1

White wine (optional) ..................... ½ cup
Pepper corns ..................................... 10-12
Bay leaves ..................................................... 2

**For garnishing**

Cabbage ........................................... shredded
Tomato ............................................................ 1
Capsicum ........................................................ 1

### METHOD OF PREPARATION

**Chef's Tip:**

*Steam the fish with slices of lemon pressed into the flesh for better flavour.*

1. Clean and wash fish fillets. Marinate with one teaspoon lemon juice and salt to taste and keep aside.
2. Peel ginger, wash and thinly slice. Peel garlic. Wash and trim spring onion, cut into round slices. Separate onion rings. Wash and cut celery into small dices. Slice lemon into roundels.
3. Mix white wine with sliced ginger, whole garlic, pepper corns, diced celery, spring onion roundels, bay leaves, lemon slices, salt and half cup water. Soak fish slices in this marinade and refrigerate for half an hour.
4. Transfer fish slices gently into a flat ovenproof dish and pour the marinade over this. Cover with a tight fitting lid or aluminum foil. Cook in a preheated oven at 220 degrees Celsius for twelve to fifteen minutes until the fish slices are just cooked.
5. Alternately it can be cooked in a steam pot for ten to twelve minutes or microwave oven for four minutes on HIGH.
6. Serve immediately with the cooking liquor, garnished with shredded cabbage, tomato and capsicum.

### NUTRITIONAL INFORMATION

| Calories | Proteins | Fat | Carbohydrates | Fibre |
|---|---|---|---|---|
| 165 | 15.6 | 0.8 | 7.4 | 0. 7 |

It is quite common to eat fish in fried form. It is also known that fish is good for the heart, because of their omega-3, fatty acids. However eating fish in the fried form can do more harm, because of the excess fat used for frying. It is hence suggested that we need to change our methods of cooking (for example steaming), for health benefits.

# METHI WALI

## *Machchi*

### INGREDIENTS

Boneless fish .................................. 4 fillets
Lemon juice .................................. 1 tblspn
Salt .................................................. to taste
*Methi* leaves .......... 1 medium sized bundle
Ginger ..................................... 1 inch knob
Garlic ........................................ 3-4 cloves
Raw Mango .................... 1 medium sized
Tomato ............................ 1 medium sized
Green chillies ......................................... 3-4
Spring onions ......................................... 3-4
Oil ........................................................ 2 tspn
Mustard seeds ............................... ½ tspn

### METHOD OF PREPARATION

1. Clean, wash and cut fish into one inch sized pieces. Marinate the fish pieces in lemon juice and salt.
2. Clean, wash and chop *methi* leaves. Peel and finely chop ginger and garlic. Wash, peel, remove seed and roughly chop the raw mango.
3. Wash tomato and finely chop. Wash green chillies, remove stem and chop. Wash, trim and chop the spring onions with the leaves.
4. Heat oil in a non-stick pan, add the mustard seeds and stir briefly till it starts crackling. Add chopped ginger and garlic, stir-fry for a minute.
5. Add chopped onion and cook over high heat till onion turns translucent. Add chopped *methi* leaves, green chillies and cook for two minutes, stirring continuously. Add chopped tomato and raw mangoes. Stir and add one cup water and continue cooking over high heat for six to eight minutes, stirring frequently.
6. Add marinated fish and salt to taste. Cover and simmer over medium heat for three to four minutes or until fish is cooked.
7. Stir gently, check and adjust seasoning and serve hot.

### NUTRITIONAL INFORMATION

| Calories | Proteins | Fat | Carbohydrates | Fibre |
|---|---|---|---|---|
| 135 | 9. 2 | 2. 5 | 9. 5 | 1. 2 |

Salt is an important ingredient from the point of view of health, though it supplies no calories. Salt (sodium in salt, to be more specific) plays an significant role in the maintenance of blood pressure. Today salt is more commonly known as iodized salt because of its iodine fortification. Iodine deficiency has serious implications. Iodine deficiency during the fetal stage may lead to mental retardation and in later life retardation of body growth. It is characterized by the swelling of thyroid gland in the neck.

# PRAWN SHASLIK WITH

## *Apple Curry Sauce*

### INGREDIENTS

Peeled deveined prawns....12-16 medium sized
Curry powder .................................. 1 tspn
Crushed pepper corn ........................ 1 tspn
Salt................................................ to taste
Lemon juice ................................. 2 tblspns
Capsicum ......................... 2 medium sized
Tomatoes ......................... 2 medium sized
Onions ............................. 2 medium sized

**For sauce**

Onion.................................1 medium sized
Ginger ..................................... 1 inch knob
Green apples .................. 2 medium sized
Lemon juice ................................. 1 tblspn
Oil .............................................. 1 tblspn
Bay leaf............................................... 1
Curry powder ................................ 2 tspns
White pepper powder......................¼ tspn
Salt............................................. to taste

### METHOD OF PREPARATION

**For shaslik**

1. Wash and pat dry the prawns and marinate them in curry powder, crushed pepper corn, salt and lemon juice and refrigerate until required.
2. Wash, halve, deseed capsicum and cut into one inch sized squared pieces.
3. Wash and cut the tomatoes in quarters, deseed and cut each quarter into two.
4. Peel and cut onions into quarters and separate onion segments.
5. Mix capsicum, tomato and onion pieces with the marinated prawns and refrigerate for fifteen to twenty minutes.
6. Skewer the marinated prawns and vegetables on a eight inch wooden skewer.
7. Heat a non-stick *tawa*, brush with a little oil and place the skewered prawns.
8. Cook them on medium heat, turning occasionally, for five to six minutes or till prawns are just done.
9. Serve hot topped with apple curry sauce.

**For sauce**

1. Peel and roughly chop onion and ginger. Wash, core and roughly chop the green apples. Mix the apple with lemon juice to prevent discolouration.
2. Heat oil in a non-stick pan, add bay leaf, chopped onion and ginger. Cook on high heat, stirring continuously, for three to four minutes or till it just starts turning brown. Add chopped green apples with one cup water and boil.
3. Reduce heat and simmer for five to six minutes or till the apples are cooked and soft.
4. Add curry powder, white pepper powder and salt to taste. Cool, remove the bay leaf and puree the apple mixture. Pass it through a sieve and keep warm.

**NUTRITIONAL INFORMATION**

| Calories | Proteins | Fat | Carbohydrates | Fibre |
|---|---|---|---|---|
| 175 | 13. 3 | 5. 2 | 19. 2 | 1. 6 |

Bay leaf, termed *Tejpatta* in Hindi is one of the most sought after culinary spices for flavouring soups, casseroles, stews and so on. Bay leaf is used to treat hysteria, amnenorrhea, piles, gas, colic and indigestion. It is known to stimulate appetite and promote digestion. It works extremely well in cases of skin rashes and skin irritations, either taken internally or by external application in the form of paste.

# POMFRET

## *Ambotic*

### INGREDIENTS

Pomfret ........ 8 slices
Turmeric powder ........ 1 tspn
Salt ........ to taste
Onions ........ 2 medium sized
Green chillies ........ 4-5
Ginger ........ 1 inch knob
Garlic ........ 8-10 cloves
Cumin seeds ........ 1 tspn
Coriander seeds ........ 1 tblspn
Grated coconut ........ 2 tblspns
Dried whole red chillies ........ 4
Cloves ........ 5
Cinnamon ........ 2 inch
White vinegar ........ 2 tblspns
Oil ........ 1 ½ tspn
Thin coconut milk ........ ¾ cup
*Kokum* water ........ 3 tblspns

### METHOD OF PREPARATION

1. Clean pomfret slices, wash thoroughly and remove excess water by gently pressing on clean and absorbent kitchen towel.
2. Marinate these slices with turmeric powder, salt and leave aside for fifteen minutes.
3. Peel and finely chop onions. Wash green chillies, remove stem and slit them. Peel and wash ginger. Peel garlic.
4. Grind together cumin seeds, coriander seeds, grated coconut, dry whole red chillies, ginger, garlic, cloves, cinnamon stick with white vinegar to a fine paste.
5. Heat oil in a non-stick pan, add chopped onion and fry till light golden brown.
6. Add ground paste and cook on medium heat for two minutes.
7. Add two cups of water and bring it to a boil. Add marinated fish, slit green chillies and cook on high heat for two to three minutes or until the fish pieces are almost cooked.
8. Stir in thin coconut milk and *kokum* water, add salt and mix gently. Reduce heat and simmer for three to four minutes.
9. Serve hot with steamed unpolished rice.

### NUTRITIONAL INFORMATION

| Calories | Proteins | Fat | Carbohydrates | Fibre |
|---|---|---|---|---|
| 195 | 11. 6 | 12. 3 | 8. 9 | 1 |

Cinnamon is known to raise vitality. It warms and stimulates all the vital functions of the body. It is known to counteract congestion, and is anti-rheumatic, stops diarrhea, improves digestion, relieves abdominal spasms and aids peripheral circulation of the blood.

# SHRIMP STUFFED

## *Pomfret*

### INGREDIENTS

Whole Pomfret fish .................................. 2
(approx. 300 gms each)
Salt .................................................. to taste
Lemon juice ................................. 2 tblspns
Crushed pepper corn ..................... 2 tspns
Ginger ..................................... 1 inch piece
Garlic ........................................ 4-6 cloves
Pepper corn ........................................ 1 tspn
Spring Onion .................. 1 medium sized
Dried thyme ...................................... ½ tspn
Peeled deveined shrimps ....... 4-6 medium sized
Oil .................................................... 2 tspns

### METHOD OF PREPARATION

1. The fish would be served whole therefore the fins should be trimmed first. Trim the tail as well.
2. Slit the stomach horizontally, carefully loosen the stomach contents from the cavity and pull them out. Clean the cavity by washing it thoroughly.
3. Take a very sharp knife and continue the slit to the tail end. With the knife tip, slowly ease away the flesh from the bone without damaging or rupturing the skin.
4. Turn the fish over and repeat the same process but starting this time from the tail end. Snip the center bone near the head and then near the tail. Gently loosen the bone and pull it out. Check for any loose bone and pull it out gently.
5. Mix salt, lemon juice and crushed pepper corns and apply this inside the boneless pomfret. Refrigerate for fifteen minutes.
6. Wash and peel ginger. Peel garlic.
7. Make a coarse paste of peeled ginger, garlic, pepper corn, spring onion, salt, dried thyme and deveined shrimps.
8. Stuff half the quantity of shrimp mixture into the pomfret. Repeat with the other pomfret similarly.
9. Cook the stuffed pomfret on a hot non-stick *tawa* on both sides with a little oil for two minutes, reduce heat, cook for three to four minutes on both sides, covered with a dome shaped lid so that the fish cooks faster.

### NUTRITIONAL INFORMATION

| Calories | Proteins | Fat | Carbohydrates | Fibre |
|---|---|---|---|---|
| 105 | 17. 7 | 3 | 2. 6 | 0. 5 |

Pomfret is also known as butter fish and is well known sea water fish. Though known as butter fish it has low fat content (1.5-2.5%) and high protein, riboflavin and niacin content. It comes in to two varieties, black and white. The black variety has more iron. Like all other fishes this variety has therapeutic role in atherosclerosis.

# PRAWNS
*Provencale*

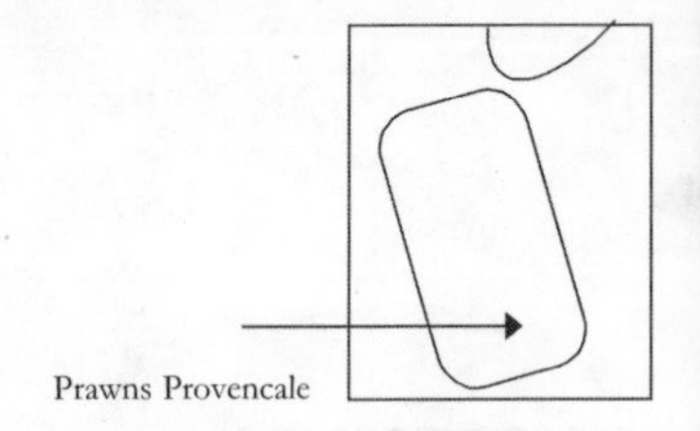
Prawns Provencale

## INGREDIENTS

Prawns, shelled ........ 12-16 medium sized
Lemon juice .................................... 2 tspns
Salt ................................................ to taste
Onions ............................ 2 medium sized
Garlic ........................................ 6-8 cloves
Fresh parsley ....................... 1 small bunch
Tomatoes ...................... 6-7 medium sized
Olive oil ............................................ 1 tspn
Bay leaf ................................................. 1
Crushed pepper corn .................... ½ tspn

## METHOD OF PREPARATION

1. Devein prawns and wash them thoroughly. Drain the excess water.
2. Marinate prawns with lemon juice and a little salt and refrigerate till required.
3. Peel and finely chop onions and garlic.
4. Clean, wash, reserve a few sprigs for garnish and finely chop the remaining parsley.
5. Wash, remove the eye of the tomatoes and make a small incision at the bottom. Boil water and blanch the tomatoes for half a minute and remove immediately. Cool, peel, cut into halves and squeeze out seeds and finely chop peeled tomatoes.
6. Heat olive oil in a non-stick pan, add bay leaf and chopped garlic. Stir-fry for half a minute.
7. Add chopped onion and cook on medium heat, stirring continuously, till onions turn translucent.
8. Add blanched chopped tomatoes. Add three fourth cups of water, cover and cook on medium heat for five minutes, stir occasionally.
9. Add marinated prawns, salt and crushed pepper corn. Stir and cook over medium heat for three to four minutes or till prawns are just cooked. Add chopped parsley and mix well.
10. Serve hot garnished with parsley sprigs.

## NUTRITIONAL INFORMATION

| Calories | Proteins | Fat | Carbohydrates | Fibre |
|---|---|---|---|---|
| 140 | 16. 3 | 5 | 8. 5 | 1. 1 |

Garlic is known for its usefulness in reducing the chances of clot formation and therefore it plays a critical role in fighting heart diseases. Garlic also has anti-bacterial properties and it inhibits the growth of harmful bacteria that cause gas formation and upset stomach.

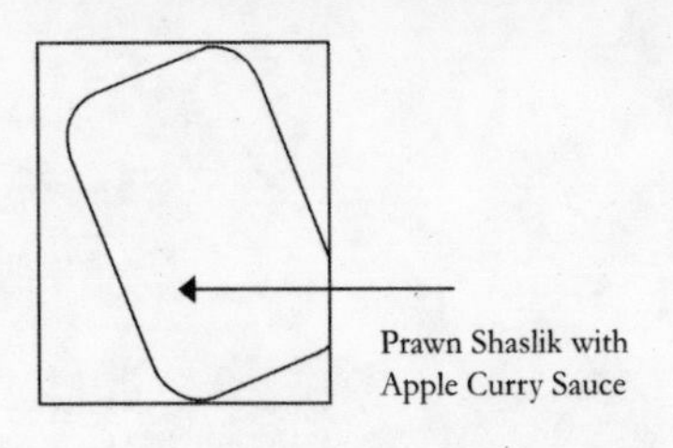

Prawn Shaslik with Apple Curry Sauce

# CHICKEN

Chicken preparations are favourite foods of many. It is associated with feast days, social and families get together.

**Nutritive Value:** Poultry meat of high quality contains 56-71% water. The edible portion has 18-22% protein. Carbohydrate content is less than one percent. The fat varies with the kind, age and quality of the bird. In addition the dark meat is slightly higher in fat content than the white meat. Poultry as a rule is lower in fat than other organ meat and hence when cooked rightly can be eaten by those on a low calorie, low fat diet. 100 gms. of lean meat has about 6 gms. of fat while the same amount of chicken without the skin (which contains most of the fat) contains about 3 gms. of fat.

Chicken is also a good source of iron, phosphorous and B complex vitamins, especially niacin. White meat has more niacin content.

The digestibility as well as rapidity and ease of digestion is another plus point for promoting chicken as a healthy food. Meat has more of yellow connective tissue (elastin), which does not tenderize on cooking. Chicken has more of white connective tissue (collagen) and cooking does make it tender and soft.

Low fat content and easy digestibility scores chicken more than meat from health point.

It is important to choose chicken from a standard place to be sure of the quality. The way chicken is reared is of great importance. A few rules to check the quality are:----

The bird's skin should be light coloured and moist (the yellow colour of some chicken shows only that they have been fed yellow foodstuffs) and the breast meat should be plump. Fresh meat is preferable to frozen, but is of uttermost important.

Poultry are particularly susceptible to salmonella bacteria, which cause food poisoning. It must be chilled properly during storage. Equipment and hands should be washed after handling the raw flesh. Frozen birds must be completely thawed before cooking. All birds should be brought to room temperature before cooking and ensure that heat penetrates thoroughly to kill the salmonella.

# CHICKEN BREAST

*Veronique*

**INGREDIENTS**

Chicken breasts,
skinned and boned ...... 4 medium sized
White pepper powder .............. to taste
Salt ........................................ to taste
Worcestershire sauce ..................... 1 tspn
Oil ........................................... 2 tspns

**For sauce**

Green grapes (seedless) .............. 100 gms
Brown sugar ................................ 1 tblspn
Sweetlime juice .............................. 1 cup
Salt ........................................... to taste
Cracked pepper corns ..................... 1 tspn
Cornflour ...................................... 2 tspns

**METHOD OF PREPARATION**

1. Clean the chicken breasts and wash them.
2. Marinate chicken breasts in a mixture of white pepper powder, salt and Worcestershire sauce. Refrigerate until required.
3. Wash and cut half the quantity of grapes into halves and puree the rest in a blender.
4. Heat oil in a non-stick pan, place the marinated chicken breasts in it and cook on medium flame for two to three minutes, turning the chicken breasts once. Reduce heat, cover the pan and continue cooking for three to four minutes till they turn golden brown and crisp on both sides. Keep aside.
5. Take a non-stick pan and melt brown sugar mixed with sweet lime juice. Keep cooking till sugar is completely dissolved. Stir in grape puree. Season with salt and cracked pepper corns.
6. Dissolve cornflour in quarter cup water and stir this in the sauce, keep stirring continuously. Place the cooked chicken in the pan and stir in the halved grapes. Simmer for two minutes and serve hot.

**NUTRITIONAL INFORMATION**

| Calories | Proteins | Fat | Carbohydrates | Fibre |
|---|---|---|---|---|
| 220 | 25. 3 | 6.7 | 12. 7 | 1 |

Grapes come in two varieties, those with seeds and seedless. Grapes have 80% moisture and about 70 calories/100gms of raw weight. Like other fruits they hardly have any protein but have fair amount of magnesium. Dry products of grapes, like currants and raisins have a high amount of iron and fibre.

# CHICKEN PARCELS
## *in Orange Sauce*

### INGREDIENTS

| | | | |
|---|---|---|---|
| Chicken breasts, skinned | 4 medium sized | Onion | 1 small sized |
| Spinach | 20 medium sized leaves | Garlic | 5 cloves |
| Lemon juice | 1 tblspn | Low fat paneer | 75 gms |
| Worcestershire sauce | 1 tblspn | Oil | 1 tblspn |
| Mustard powder | 1 tspn | Cornflour | 2 tspns |
| White pepper powder | ½ tspn | Orange juice, preferably fresh | 1 ½ cups |
| Salt | to taste | Cinnamon powder | a pinch |

### METHOD OF PREPARATION

1. Clean, trim and lightly flatten the chicken breasts with a steak hammer. Retain the wing bone attached to the chicken breast. Mix lemon juice, Worcestershire sauce, mustard powder, white pepper powder and salt. Apply this seasoning mix evenly on the chicken breasts. Refrigerate until required.
2. Clean, wash and blanch spinach leaves for five to ten seconds in plenty of boiling water. Drain, separate the leaves and cool. Peel and finely chop onion and garlic. Grate the low fat paneer and keep.
3. Heat oil in a non-stick pan, add chopped onion and garlic. Sauté over high heat for two to three minutes or until the onion turns translucent. Add the grated low fat paneer and salt. Mix well and continue cooking for another two minutes, stirring continuously. Remove from heat and cool.
4. Divide the paneer mixture into four equal portions and roll into balls.
5. Take each chicken breast and lay four blanched spinach leaves covering the entire top surface of the chicken. Place one paneer ball on it.
6. Place the chicken breast with the filling on a 9 inch × 9 inch sheet of aluminum foil and gather into a bundle with the wing bone jutting out at the center. Twist the ends of the foil around the bone to tightly seal, ensuring that the filling does not spill out.
7. Boil sufficient water, reduce heat and poach the chicken rolls at medium heat for twenty minutes or till done.
8. Drain and remove the chicken rolls, unwrap the aluminum foil and keep warm.
9. For making the sauce, dissolve cornflour in orange juice and bring to a boil, stirring continuously. Season with salt and cinnamon powder.
10. Slice the cooked chicken pieces, each into two, and serve along with orange sauce.

### NUTRITIONAL INFORMATION

| Calories | Proteins | Fat | Carbohydrates | Fibre |
|---|---|---|---|---|
| 195 | 25. 9 | 6.4 | 7.7 | 0.3 |

Stir-frying as a method of cooking vegetables (vegetables cooked in small amount of oil in a covered pan) retain nutrients well. Water-soluble nutrients (Vitamin C, B complex and many minerals) will easily diffuse out of food into cooking water. However, water-soluble Vitamins will not diffuse in oil. It is thus recommended to stir-fry vegetables the Chinese way (cook for a short period without over cooking, in minimum amount of oil).

# COUNTRY STYLE

## *Chicken Stew*

### INGREDIENTS

Chicken, with bone..........½ medium sized
Carrot................................1 medium sized
Potato.............................. 1 medium sized
Turnip.............................. 1 medium sized
Onions....................... 6-8 very small sized
French beans......................................... 6-8
Cauliflower ....... 3-4 medium sized florets
Celery....................................... 2 inch stalk
Bay leaf.................................................... 2
Fresh parsley ............................ 6-8 sprigs
Dried thyme.................................... ½ tspn
Pepper corns, lightly crushed.............. 6-8
Oil ................................................. 1 tblspn
Garlic ........................................ 6-8 cloves
Whole meal flour ......................... 4 tblspn
Salt.............................................. to taste

### METHOD OF PREPARATION

1. Clean, wash and cut chicken into eight medium sized pieces. Peel carrot, potato, turnip and cut into three fourth inch sized pieces.
2. Peel the onions and keep them whole. Wash, string and cut French beans into one inch sized pieces. Wash and cut cauliflower into small sized florets. Crush celery stalk lightly.
3. Take a clean 6 inch × 6 inch muslin cloth and tie bay leaf, fresh parsley, celery, dried thyme and crushed pepper corn into a small bundle.
4. Heat oil in a thick bottomed pan, add crushed garlic and stir-fry briefly. Gradually add the whole meal flour, stirring constantly and cook over medium heat for a minute.
5. Add the chicken pieces and cook on high heat for three to four minutes, stirring continuously.
6. Reduce heat and add the cut potatoes, carrot, turnip, French beans, cauliflower and peeled onions. Mix well and add four cups of water.
7. Stir to mix thoroughly, add salt to taste and the muslin cloth bundle with the herbs and spices. Bring to a boil, stirring frequently.
8. Reduce the heat, cover with a tight fitting lid and simmer for ten to twelve minutes or until the chicken is completely cooked and the stew has thickened lightly.
9. Remove the muslin cloth bundle, adjust seasoning and serve steaming hot.

#### NUTRITIONAL INFORMATION

| Calories | Proteins | Fat | Carbohydrates | Fibre |
|---|---|---|---|---|
| 200 | 17. 8 | 6.8 | 16. 4 | 1.1 |

Celery leaves are high in B-carotene and niacin. Niacin is commonly known as B3 Vitamin. It is concerned with carbohydrate, fat and protein metabolism in the body. It is water-soluble and cannot be stored in the body. The deficiency of this Vitamin in the diet is characterized by soreness of tongue, pigmented skin and diarrhea. Whole cereals, pulses, nuts and meat are good sources of Niacin. Groundnut is particularly rich in Niacin.

# FARM HOUSE LETTUCE

*Roll*

## INGREDIENTS

Iceberg lettuce ............................ 8 leaves
Garlic .................................... 10-12 cloves
Onion ........................... 1 medium sized
Melon seeds ................................. 1 tblspn
Oil ...................................................... 1 tspn
Chicken mince ........................... 300 gms
Black bean sauce ......................... 1 tblspn
Salt ................................................... to taste
Sugar ................................................. ½ tspn
Crushed black pepper .................... to taste

## METHOD OF PREPARATION

1. Wash iceberg lettuce leaves thoroughly and keep them in iced water.
2. Peel, crush and chop garlic. Peel and finely chop onion. Dry roast melon seeds in a heated non stick pan till slightly browned.
3. Heat oil in a non-stick pan, add chopped garlic and onion and cook till onion turns soft and translucent.
4. Add chicken mince and cook on high heat stirring continuously. for about three to four minutes.
5. Stir in black bean sauce, salt, sugar and crushed black pepper. Mix well.
6. Cook covered on a low flame till chicken mince is fully cooked. Remove from flame. Add roasted melon seeds and mix well.
7. Remove the lettuce leaves from iced water, shake off excess water. Arrange on a serving dish.
8. Put two spoonfuls of cooked chicken mince on each lettuce leaf and lightly roll and secure with a wooden toothpick. Serve immediately.

### NUTRITIONAL INFORMATION

| Calories | Proteins | Fat | Carbohydrates | Fibre |
|---|---|---|---|---|
| 195 | 23. 9 | 8. 5 | 4. 2 | 0. 3 |

Lettuce, commonly known as salad leaves is one of the leafy vegetable eaten raw. Hence it is possible to retain nutrients like Vitamin C and B complex, which otherwise are destroyed by heat. It is also a good source of choline, calcium and B-carotene. Lettuce can be incorporated into many dishes to give more bulk and fibre, without adding more calories

# MURGH SABZ

*Resham*

## INGREDIENTS

Chicken breasts, skinless & boneless ........ 3
Onions ........ 2 medium sized
Tomatoes ........ 2 medium sized
Capsicum ........ 2 medium sized
Ginger ........ 2 one inch knobs
Garlic ........ 6-8 cloves
Green chillies ........ 2
Fresh coriander leaves ........ ¼ cup
Oil ........ 1 tspn
Cumin seeds ........ 1 tspn
Curry leaves ........ ½ tspn
Turmeric powder ........ ½ tspn
Red chilli powder ........ 1 tspn
Salt ........ to taste
*Garam masala* powder ........ 1 tspn
Lemon juice ........ 1 tblspn

## METHOD OF PREPARATION

1. Clean, wash and cut chicken breasts into finger sized pieces. Peel, halve and cut onion into thick slices. Separate the different layers of onion. Wash, halve, remove seeds and cut tomatoes and capsicum into ling strips of half cm width.
2. Peel and cut ginger into julienne. Peel and finely chop garlic. Wash, remove stem and slit green chillies into two. Wash and finely chop fresh coriander leaves.
3. Heat oil in a non-stick pan and add cumin seeds. When it starts to change colour, add curry leaves, chopped garlic and slit green chillies. Stir-fry briefly and add onions. Cook on medium heat for half a minute, stirring frequently.
4. Add chicken pieces and continue to cook on medium heat for five minutes, stirring occasionally. Add turmeric powder, red chilli powder and salt. Mix well.
5. Add capsicum and ginger julienne. Cook on medium heat for two minutes, stirring occasionally. Sprinkle *garam masala* powder and lemon juice. Mix well and add tomatoes. Reduce heat and continue to further for two minutes.
6. Serve hot, garnished with chopped coriander leaves.

### NUTRITIONAL INFORMATION

| Calories | Proteins | Fat | Carbohydrates | Fibre |
|---|---|---|---|---|
| 180 | 24.4 | 6.5 | 7.2 | 0.9 |

Typically Indian, curry leaves have curryish scent and flavour minus the chilli content. They are high in calcium, beta-carotene, folic acid, zinc and choline. They can be used fresh, dried, whole, chopped or pounded.

# MURGH

## *Makkai*

**INGREDIENTS**

Chicken breasts,
skinless & boneless ......... 4 medium sized
Capsicum ......................... 2 medium sized
Ginger ..................................... 1 inch knob
Garlic .......................................... 5-6 cloves
Tomatoes ......................... 3 medium sized
Fresh coriander leaves .................... ½ cup
Corn kernels ........................................ 1 cup
Oil ........................................... 1½ tblspn
Red chilli powder ............................ 1 tspn
Turmeric powder ............................ ½ tspn
Coriander powder ........................ 1 tblspn
Skimmed milk yogurt ................. 2 tblspns
Salt ............................................... to taste
*Garam masala* powder ..................... ½ tspn

**METHOD OF PREPARATION**

1. Clean, wash and cut chicken breasts into one inch sized square pieces.
2. Wash capsicum, halve, deseed and cut into one cm. sized square pieces. Peel and finely chop ginger and garlic. Wash and puree tomatoes in a blender. Wash and chop green coriander.
3. Boil corn kernels in three to four cups of salted water till soft. Drain and keep aside.
4. Heat oil in a non-stick pan, stir-fry chopped ginger and garlic briefly. Add pureed tomato and cook on medium high heat, stirring frequently.
5. Stir in red chilli powder, turmeric powder and coriander powder. Mix well. Add chicken pieces and cook on medium heat for five to six minutes, stirring regularly.
6. Add skimmed milk yogurt, cooked corn kernels, capsicum and salt. Mix well, reduce heat, cover and continue to cook till masala is a little thick and chicken pieces are completely cooked.
7. Add *garam masala* powder and chopped coriander leaves, mix gently and serve hot.

**NUTRITIONAL INFORMATION**

| Calories | Proteins | Fat | Carbohydrates | Fibre |
|---|---|---|---|---|
| 225 | 26. 6 | 9 | 7. 9 | 1 |

Capsicum is also known as giant chilli or bell pepper. Because of high moisture and low fat content it is a low calorie vegetable. It has fair amount of B-carotene and Vitamin C. Green chillies also have good amount of B-carotene and Vitamin C, but amount consumed is very less due to their pungent taste. Capsicum, which is not pungent, can be used in more quantities as a substitute for green chillies, to supply additional B-carotene and Vitamin C.

# SESAME SOYA

## *Chicken*

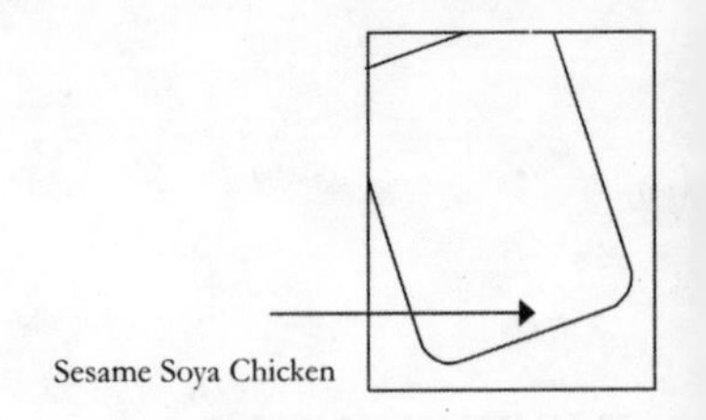
Sesame Soya Chicken

### INGREDIENTS

Chicken breasts, skinless & boneless ..... 4
Garlic .......................................... 5-6 cloves
Spring onion .................... 1 medium sized
Dried whole red chillies ........................... 2
White sesame seeds ....................... 2 tspns
Cornflour ...................................... 1 tblspn
Oil ....................................................... 1 tspn
Dark soya sauce ........................... 2 tblspns
Salt..................................................... to taste
Port wine (optional) .................... 2 tblspns
White vinegar ................................ 1 tblspn
Sesame oil ........................................... 1 tspn

### METHOD OF PREPARATION

1. Clean, wash and cut chicken breasts into one inch dices.
2. Peel and finely chop garlic. Wash, trim and finely chop spring onion. Slice spring onion greens and reserve for garnish. Wash, pat dry and thinly slice dried red chillies.
3. Roast white sesame seeds on to a warm griddle until slightly browned. Dissolve cornflour in quarter cup water. Keep aside.
4. Heat oil in a non-stick pan, add finely chopped garlic and spring onion and stir-fry briefly. Stir in dark soya sauce and thinly sliced dried red chillies.
5. Immediately add chicken pieces and continue cooking on high heat, stirring continuously. Stir in Port wine and one cup of water, bring it to a boil. Cook for one minute, stirring frequently.
6. Stir in cornflour dissolved in water while stirring continuously. Simmer for two to three minutes. Add salt, white vinegar and sesame oil. Mix well.
7. Serve hot topped and garnished with roasted sesame seeds and sliced spring onion leaves.

### NUTRITIONAL INFORMATION

| Calories | Proteins | Fat | Carbohydrates | Fibre |
|---|---|---|---|---|
| 245 | 26. 3 | 13. 2 | 2. 8 | 0.4 |

Sesame seeds (*Til*) is one of those oil seeds which is not only rich in proteins and fat, but also very high in calcium, phosphorous and iron. Children, pregnant and lactating mothers should be encouraged to eat products made with sesame seeds.

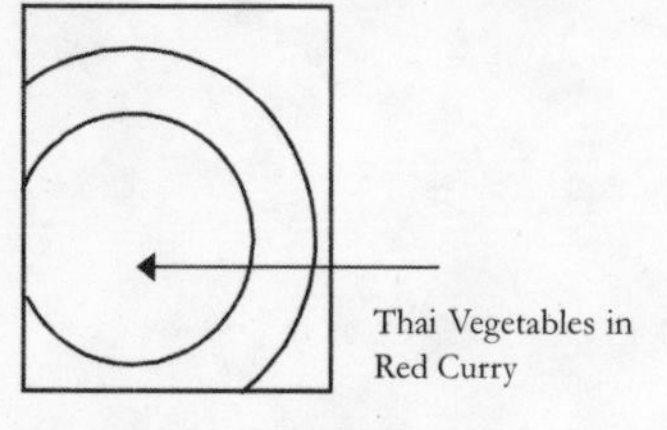


# SPICED CHICKEN
*Bites*

## INGREDIENTS

Chicken, skinless & boneless ... 400 gms
Onion ... 1 medium sized
Ginger ... 1 inch knob
Garlic ... 4 cloves
Green chillies ... 3-4
Cumin seeds ... 2 tspns
Coriander seeds ... 1 tblspn
Pepper corns ... 1 tspn
Cloves ... 3-4
Cinnamon ... 1 inch stick
Lemon juice ... 1 tblspn
Oil ... 2 tblspns
Salt ... to taste

## METHOD OF PREPARATION

1. Clean, wash and cut chicken into bite sized (half inch) dices.
2. Peel, wash and roughly slice onion and ginger. Peel garlic. Wash green chillies, remove stems and cut into two.
3. Dry roast cumin seeds, coriander seeds, pepper corns, cloves and cinnamon.
4. Mix together sliced onion, ginger, green chillies, garlic, lemon juice and roasted cumin seeds, coriander seeds, peppercorn, cloves and cinnamon. Grind them to a fine paste.
5. Marinate chicken pieces in this paste for two hours in the refrigerator.
6. Heat oil in a non-stick pan and cook the marinated chicken pieces on medium heat for five minutes, stirring continuously. Add salt and mix well.
7. Reduce heat, cover and cook on low heat for five minutes or till chicken pieces are fully cooked, stirring occasionally. Serve hot.

## NUTRITIONAL INFORMATION

| Calories | Proteins | Fat | Carbohydrates | Fibre |
|---|---|---|---|---|
| 270 | 31. 4 | 13. 9 | 3. 3 | 0. 2 |

Onion is a commonly used bulb vegetable. One medium sized onion would give about 50-60 calories. Onions are used to treat stomach disorders, kidney diseases and inflammation. They contain oils of sulphur compound and flavonoids, which are known to protect the heart.

# GREEK STYLE

## *Yogurt Chicken*

### INGREDIENTS

Chicken Breasts, ........................................ 4
(skinless and boneless)
Skimmed milk yogurt ...................... ½ cup
Parsley .................................... 1 small sprig
Fresh coriander leaves ...................... 15-20
Fresh mint leaves .............................. 10-12
Garlic ........................................ 8-10 cloves
Lemon juice .................................... 2 tblspn
Olive oil ..................................... 1 ½ tblspn
Paprika powder .................................. ½ tspn
Black pepper (crushed) .................. ½ tspn
Salt ................................................ to taste
Oil .................................................... 1 tspn
Black olives ............................................ 6-8

### METHOD OF PREPARATION

1. Clean the chicken breasts and make three slits on each breast piece.
2. Hang the skimmed milk yogurt in a muslin cloth for about ten to fifteen minutes to drain the excess liquid. Whisk the thickened yogurt and keep aside.
3. Wash and finely chop the parsley, coriander and mint, separately. Peel and grind garlic to a fine paste.
4. Mix the lemon juice with yogurt, garlic paste, olive oil, paprika powder, pepper, salt to taste and half the chopped fresh parsley, coriander and mint.
5. Marinate the chicken in this mixture and refrigerate. Let it marinate for an hour.
6. Heat a non-stick shallow pan and brush a little oil.
7. Add the chicken breast pieces and sear them on high heat for one minute on either side.
8. Reduce the heat, cover and cook the chicken turning occasionally for uniform cooking and browning.
9. Cook for about eight to ten minutes or until completely cooked. Add the black olives at the last stage, stir and turn out into a serving dish.
10. Garnish with the remaining chopped herbs and serve hot.

**Chef's Tip:**

*You may substitute paprika powder with red chilli powder that is not too hot and is bright red in colour, eg. Kashmiri Chilli Powder or Deghi Mirch.*

### NUTRITIONAL INFORMATION

| Calories | Proteins | Fat | Carbohydrates | Fibre |
|---|---|---|---|---|
| 245 | 31.6 | 8.8 | 1.1 | 0.1 |

Buttermilk is known to be a healthy drink since ancient India. Regular use of buttermilk tonifies the small intestine and can alleviate hemorrhoids. Thin buttermilk is low in calories (30 cals/glass). If made from skimmed milk it will be even lower.

In contrast to thin buttermilk, *lassi* is a high calorie drink but is also high in proteins, calcium and Vitamin A and can be an excellent drink for children. However, due to the butter, salt or sugar present in *lassi*, buttermilk makes a better drink for weight watchers, diabetics and those with high blood pressure.

# HANDI *Murgh*

## INGREDIENTS

Chicken ........................ ½ medium sized
Onion ........................ 2 medium sized
Poppy seeds ........................ 2 tblspns
Tomatoes ........................ 2 medium sized
Ginger ........................ 2 one inch knobs
Garlic ........................ 10-12 cloves
Green Chillies ........................ 4-5
Fresh coriander leaves ........................ ½ cup
Mint leaves ........................ ¼ cup
Fenugreek seeds ........................ 1 tspn
Fennel seeds ........................ 1 tspn
Coriander seeds ........................ 2 tblspns
Cumin seeds ........................ 1 tspn
Skimmed milk yogurt ........................ ¼ cup
Salt ........................ to taste
Turmeric powder ........................ ½ tspn
*Garam masala* powder ........................ 1 tspn

## METHOD OF PREPARATION

1. Clean, remove skin and cut chicken into eight medium sized pieces with the bone.
2. Peel onion and finely grate. Clean, wash and soak the poppy seeds in quarter cup warm water for fifteen to twenty minutes.
3. Wash and cut tomatoes into four. Peel ginger and garlic and roughly chop.
4. Wash, remove stem and roughly chop green chillies, fresh coriander and mint leaves. Grind the green chillies, chopped fresh coriander and mint leaves with the ginger, garlic and soaked poppy seeds to a fine and smooth paste.
5. Dry roast the fenugreek seeds, fennel seeds, coriander seeds and cumin seeds lightly on a *tawa* and grind to a powder.
6. Mix the chicken pieces, green masala paste, skimmed milk yogurt, salt to taste, turmeric powder, freshly ground dry spice powder and the *garam masala* powder.
7. Refrigerate and leave to marinate for an hour.
8. Place the chicken in a thick-bottomed *handi* (a vessel with a narrow opening), mix in the grated onion, tomatoes and half cup water.
9. Seal the *handi* with a tight fitting lid or with whole wheat (*atta*) dough. Keep the *handi* on medium heat and cook for eight to ten minutes.
10. Reduce heat and place the *handi* on a hot *tawa* and simmer for ten to fifteen minutes. Alternately you can cook in a preheated oven at 160 degrees Celcius for fifteen minutes.
11. Break the seal and open the *handi* carefully just before serving to retain the flavour and aroma.

## NUTRITIONAL INFORMATION

| Calories | Proteins | Fat | Carbohydrates | Fibre |
|---|---|---|---|---|
| 180 | 24.8 | 4.9 | 7.4 | 0.8 |

Poppy seeds are commonly known as khus-khus. They are a rich source of many nutrients. They have around 21% protein and extremely high in calcium, phosphorous and iron. They are also very rich in trace elements like magnesium, manganese, zinc and chromium.

# TAMATAR MURGH

*Kofta*

## INGREDIENTS

Chicken breast, skinless & boneless ... 4-5
Ginger .......... 2 one inch knobs
Garlic .......... 5-6 cloves
Green chillies .......... 2
Fresh coriander leaves .......... ¼ cup
Tomatoes .......... 5-6 medium sized
Onion .......... 1 medium sized
Curry leaves .......... 8-10
Red chilli powder .......... 1 tspn
Coriander powder .......... 2 tspns
Cumin powder .......... 1 tspn
Salt .......... to taste
Oil .......... 1 tspns
Mustard seeds .......... ½ tspn
Rice flour .......... 2 tspns
*Garam masala* powder .......... ½ tspn

## METHOD OF PREPARATION

1. Clean, trim and roughly cut chicken breasts into small pieces.
2. Peel and grind ginger and garlic to a fine paste.
3. Wash green chillies, remove stems and roughly chop. Wash, drain and roughly chop fresh coriander. Wash tomatoes and cut into quarters. Peel onion and roughly slice. Wash and pat dry curry leaves.
4. Mince chicken pieces along with chopped green chillies, half of the chopped coriander leaves and salt. Ensuring that the mince is smooth and fine divide minced chicken into ten to twelve equal portions, shape them into balls and refrigerate till required.
5. Pressure cook tomatoes for five to six minutes, along with onion, ginger-garlic paste, remaining coriander leaves, red chilli powder, coriander powder, cumin powder, salt and one cup water.
6. Leave it aside for fifteen minutes and then open the pressure cooker. Bring the contents to room temperature and puree them to a fine paste
7. Heat oil in pan, add mustard seeds and when they start to crackle, add curry leaves. Stir-fry briefly. Stir in pureed tomato mixture, one-cup water and bring it to a boil.
8. Reduce heat and gently slide in prepared chicken balls. Cover the pan with a tight fitting lid and simmer for fifteen minutes.
9. Dissolve rice flour in quarter cup water and add to the gravy, stirring continuously. Simmer for five minutes and add *garam masala* powder.

### NUTRITIONAL INFORMATION

| Calories | Proteins | Fat | Carbohydrates | Fibre |
|---|---|---|---|---|
| 190 | 24. 8 | 5.6 | 8. 8 | 1. 1 |

Coriander seeds and other spices contain a good amount of folic acid. Folic acid is present in both animal and plant foods. Fresh green vegetables, liver, pulses are good sources of this Vitamin. Folic acid is required for the multiplication of red blood cells. Apart from iron deficiency, anemia can also result from the deficiency of folic acid, which is often seen in children and pregnant women.

# ACCOMPANIMENTS

Typically though accompaniments may seem to be an insignificant part of a complete meal, in actuality have a meaningful contribution in our diet. Accompaniments are usually dishes which are simple and minor in nature, but play a very important role in making the dish it accompanies or the meal itself complete and satisfying to all the senses of sight, smell and taste.

An accompaniment provides variety and improves the nutritive value of the meal by contributing all the necessary nutrients that may be lacking in the main dish or the meal. An accompaniment is usually determined by custom based on the intention to improve the overall suitability of the dish or the entire meal.

These can be broadly classified as vegetables, cereals, pulses or starch. The most important role of the accompaniment is the balancing act it plays to the main dish or meal. Serve a protein rich main dish with a dish high in fiber or starch, thereby providing a balanced meal. Similarly to give variety to the taste buds, accompany a spicy dish with a soothing cereal or a lightly seasoned vegetable. Give a visual feast by choosing an accompaniment that contrasts with colour to the main dish. Accompaniments may either be complementing or contrasting in nature. In any role they cannot be ignored.

At times due to their constituents, an accompaniment can take the role of the main dish itself to provide a light meal or to satisfy a diet requirement.

So the modern proverb goes, "A dish's character is determined by the company it keeps".

# DALIA AUR DAL

## *Parantha*

### INGREDIENTS

Green chillies ............. 1-2 medium sized
Fresh coriander leaves .................... ½ cup
Ginger.................................... 1 inch knob
Whole wheat flour (*Atta*) ................ 1 cup
Salt ................................................ to taste
Cracked wheat (*Dalia* or *lapsi*) .......... ¾ cup
Whole *moong* .................................... ¼ cup
Oil ................................................ 2 tspns

### METHOD OF PREPARATION

1. Wash green chillies, remove stem and finely chop. Wash coriander leaves and chop them fine. Peel ginger and finely grate.
2. Combine whole wheat flour and salt.
3. Pick whole *moong*, wash well and then soak for about an hour. Drain and leave aside.
4. Clean *dalia* well. Pressure cook whole *moong* and *dalia* in one and half cups of water until soft. Cool and mash the mixture.
5. Mix wheat flour with cooked whole *moong* and *dalia*, add water, if required, a little at a time and knead into a soft and pliable dough along with grated ginger, chopped coriander leaves and green chillies.
6. Keep the dough covered with a moist cloth for fifteen minutes.
7. Divide the dough into eight to ten equal portions. Form them into balls (*pedas*). Roll out each portion to thin five to six inches sized discs.
8. Brush a little oil on a hot non stick griddle(*tawa*) and place the *parantha* on it and cook on medium heat for half a minute on each side. Reduce heat and cook further till both the sides are slightly browned.

### NUTRITIONAL INFORMATION

| Calories | Proteins | Fat | Carbohydrates | Fibre |
|---|---|---|---|---|
| 130 | 4. 1 | 4.4 | 20 | 0. 7 |

*Dalia* is broken wheat. Its preparation should be encouraged because it is more nutritious than other refined wheat products like *maida* and *rawa*. Broken wheat has more than double the amount of iron, thiamine and niacin as compared to *rawa* or *maida*. *Rawa* can be replaced by *dalia* in *upma* and other such preparations. Fibre content of *dalia* is 1.2 gms./100 gms. as compared to 0.2-0.3/100 gms. of *rawa* or *maida*. Micronutrients like magnesium, manganese and zinc are found in high quantity in cracked wheat, where as they are destroyed during the processing of wheat to *rawa* or *maida*.

# CUCUMBER

*Pachdi*

## INGREDIENTS

Cucumbers .......................... 2 small sized
Skimmed milk yogurt ................ 1 ½ cups
Ginger ...................................... ½ inch knob
Green chillies ......................................... 2-3
Grated coconut(optional) ........... 2 tblspns
Salt ................................................ to taste
Oil ...................................................... 1 tspn
Mustard seeds ................................. ½ tspn
Curry leaves ........................................ 5-6
Dried whole red chillies .......................... 2

## METHOD OF PREPARATION

1. Wash and scrub cucumbers thoroughly and then grate with the skin.
2. Pour Skimmed milk yogurt into a clean muslin cloth and hang it for half an hour, preferably in a cool place.
3. Peel, wash and finely chop ginger. Wash green chillies, remove stem and finely chop.
4. Grind together grated coconut, green chillies and ginger to a fine paste.
5. Mix together the grated cucumber, ground coconut *masala* and yogurt. Add salt to taste.
6. Heat oil in a small pan, add mustard seeds. When they start to crackle, add curry leaves, dried red chillies broken into two, stir for a moment.
7. Pour it on to the yogurt mixture. Stir it thoroughly.
8. Serve chilled.

## NUTRITIONAL INFORMATION

| Calories | Proteins | Fat | Carbohydrates | Fibre |
|---|---|---|---|---|
| 35 | 2 | 1.1 | 4. 7 | 0. 2 |

Cucumber is very low in calories since its moisture content is high. Cucumber is one vegetable, which can be eaten with skin. All fruits and vegetables, which can be eaten with the skin, should be eaten with the skin, because the skin has high fibre content and also contain more nutrients.

# MIXED FLOUR METHI

## *Chappati*

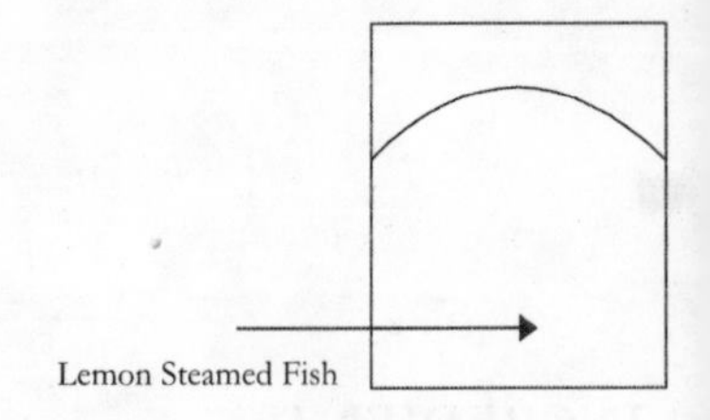


### INGREDIENTS

Bengal Gram flour (*Besan*) ............. ½ cup
Whole wheat flour (*Atta*) .............. ½ cup
Barley flour ...................................... ½ cup
Salt................................................ to taste
Fresh *methi* ......................................... 1 cup
Cabbage................................ ¼ small sized
Skimmed milk yogurt ...................... ½ cup
Red chilli powder ............................ 1 tspn

### METHOD OF PREPARATION

1. Sieve *besan*, wheat flour and barley flour along with salt.
2. Clean and wash *methi* in flowing water. Drain and finely chop the leaves. Finely grate cabbage.
3. Mix the chopped *methi* leaves and grated cabbage into the flour mixture. Add yogurt and red chilli powder. Add water, a little at a time, to make medium soft dough. Knead well.
4. Keep it covered with a moist cloth for about fifteen minutes.
5. Divide the dough into eight to ten equal portions, and roll them into balls (*pedas*).
6. Heat a non-stick griddle plate (*tawa*) to medium heat. Roll out each portion of the dough into a disc of five to six inches diameter. Place it on the hot griddle plate and cook on one side for about half a minute.
7. Flip it over and cook the other side. Reduce heat and cook on both sides on low heat till light brown.
8. Serve hot.

### NUTRITIONAL INFORMATION

| Calories | Proteins | Fat | Carbohydrates | Fibre |
|---|---|---|---|---|
| 140 | 6. 9 | 1.1 | 26. 8 | 1. 2 |

Combining cereal with pulses enhances protein quality as plant proteins are of poor quality compared to egg or milk products. A judicious combination of cereal and pulses in the ratio 5:1 has been found to improve the protein quality remarkably. Traditionally, we have been taught to eat cereal and pulses together (like *roti* with *rajma* or rice with *dal*), which indeed has a rational basis.

In this recipe too combination of cereal flour (*atta* and *barley*) with pulses (*besan*) improves the protein quality remarkably.

Sweet Corn Kadhi

Quick Pressure Cooked Vegetables

# HERB AND ONION
## *Bread*

## INGREDIENTS

Fresh Yeast .................................... 20 gms
Sugar ................................................ 1 tspn
Warm water ....................................... 1 cup
Milk ................................................... ½ cup
Butter ........................................... 4 tblspns
Onions ............................. 2 medium sized
Whole wheat flour ..................... 2½ cups
Salt ............................................. 1½ tspn
Mixed herbs ................................. 1½ tspn

## METHOD OF PREPARATION

1. Crumble yeast into a cup and sprinkle with the sugar. Add two tablespoons of warm water and mix until smooth.
2. Set in warm place for ten minutes, or until the mixture becomes frothy.
3. Pour the milk into a pan and heat gently. Remove from heat just before the milk begins to boil.
4. Chop the butter, drop into the milk then add the remaining water.
5. Leave it for ten minutes or until the butter has completely melted and the milk remain lukewarm.
6. Peel the onions and finely mince or grate them.
7. Put the flour and salt into a large basin. Add the herbs and the onion. Mix well.
8. Make a well in the center and add the yeast mixture. With a light hand make soft dough.
9. Cover with a damp cloth and leave it in a warm place for two hours, or until the dough has doubled in bulk.
10. Grease two 450 gms. bread tin. Knead the dough once again well and divide into two.
11. Shape the dough into loaves and put it into the tins. Cover and leave for fermenting for forty five minutes or until the dough is almost double.
12. Bake in a preheated oven for forty five minutes at 180 degree Celcius. Increase the heat to 220 degrees Celcius and bake for further twenty minutes.
13. Remove from the tins and cool on a wire tray. Slice and serve fresh and warm.

**Chef's Tip:**

*Use fresh herbs for better flavour and experiment with different herbs.*

## NUTRITIONAL INFORMATION

| Calories | Proteins | Fat | Carbohydrates | Fibre |
|---|---|---|---|---|
| 50 | 1. 6 | 1.2 | 8. 5 | 0. 2 |

Whole wheat bread is more nutritious since it is made from the whole grain of wheat whereas white bread is made only from the starchy endosperm. Refined flour (*maida*) lacks the bran and germ and is low in vital nutrients. Hence products made from refined flour need to be enriched with added B complex and iron. Despite this addition, whole wheat bread contains significantly more fibre, vitamin B6, folacin, magnesium and zinc than white bread. Whole grain products differ in two ways.

Whole grain bread and cereals are generally darker in colour and have a coarse texture. Also because they contain the germ, which contains oil, these turn rancid more quickly. When purchasing whole wheat bread, make sure the label states 100% Whole Wheat, which ascertains that it is truly whole grain bread. Very often, wheat breads are coloured with molasses to appear like whole wheat bread but are really white bread.

# PAUSHTIK BAJRE KI

*Roti*

## INGREDIENTS

Millet (*Bajra*) flour ........................ 1 cup
Whole wheat flour (*Atta*) ............. ¼ cup
Salt ............................................ to taste
Onion ........................... 1 medium sized
Carrot ........................... 1 medium sized
Green chillies ........................................ 2
*Ajwain* ............................................ 1 tspn

## METHOD OF PREPARATION

1. Sieve *bajra* flour, *atta* and salt together. Peel onion and grate. Wash carrot, peel and grate. Wash green chillies, remove stem and chop them finely.
2. Mix *bajra* flour, *atta* and salt mixture with grated onion, grated carrot, chopped green chillies and *ajwain*. Add water, a little at a time and knead the mixture into medium soft dough. Do not knead the dough excessively.
3. Divide the dough into eight equal portions and roll them into balls (*pedas*). Wet your palms, take a portion of dough and pat it between your palms to make thin discs of about four to five inch diameter (*rotis*). Make it as thin as possible. It takes some practice before you can make thin *bajra* rotis.
4. Heat a non-stick griddle (*tawa*) and place the *roti* on it. First cook one side for about half a minute on medium heat and then flip it over and cook the other side similarly. Reduce flame and cook on slow heat on both sides till the *bajra roti* is slightly browned.
5. Repeat the same method with the remaining dough. Serve hot.

## NUTRITIONAL INFORMATION

| Calories | Proteins | Fat | Carbohydrates | Fibre |
|---|---|---|---|---|
| 200 | 6. 3 | 2. 2 | 39. 3 | 1.1 |

One of the important nutrients that *bajra* contains is copper. Copper is involved in iron metabolism and nervous system functioning. It plays a role in the pigmentation of skin, hair and eyes. It is also required for cardiovascular and skeletal integrity.

# PALAK
## *Raita*

**INGREDIENTS**

| | | | |
|---|---|---|---|
| Spinach | 2 medium sized bundles | Skimmed milk yogurt | 2 cups |
| Spring onions | 2 medium sized | Black salt | to taste |
| Garlic | 3-4 cloves | Red chilli powder | 1 tspn |
| Green chillies | 2 | Oil | ½ tspn |
| Cumin seeds | 2 tspns | Salt | ¼ tspn |

**METHOD OF PREPARATION**

1. Clean, wash and chop spinach leaves. Clean, trim and chop spring onion with the greens. Peel and finely chop garlic. Wash, remove stem, deseed and finely chop green chillies.
2. Dry roast cumin seeds on a hot griddle plate(*tawa*) and grind to a fine powder.
3. Whisk the skimmed milk yogurt and add black salt, roasted cumin powder and red chilli powder. Mix well and chill in the refrigerator.
4. Heat oil in a non-stick pan, add chopped garlic and green chillies and stir-fry briefly. Add chopped spinach and spring onion along with its greens and sauté over high heat for three to four minutes, stirring continuously.
5. Season with salt and mix well. Continue to cook on high heat till the spinach is almost dry. Take it off the heat and cool. Mix with the seasoned yogurt just before serving.

**NUTRITIONAL INFORMATION**

| Calories | Proteins | Fat | Carbohydrates | Fibre |
|---|---|---|---|---|
| 55 | 3 | 1. 3 | 6. 6 | 0. 6 |

Cumin seeds (*jeera*) are used in every Indian household. Apart from being stimulant to our taste buds they are high in calcium, iron and phosphorous. They are also very high in choline, potassium, zinc, magnesium and manganese. Cumin seeds are used to treat digestive weakness with accompanying gas, bloat, colic and headache.

# SPICY RAJMA

## *Parantha*

### INGREDIENTS

Red kidney beans (*Rajma*) .............. $^1/_3$ cup
Green chillies .......................................... 3-4
Dry pomegranate seeds ................. ½ tspn
Mint leaves ............................................ 8-10
Whole wheat flour ............................ 1 cup
Soya flour ........................................ 2 tblspns
Red chilli powder ............................ 1 tspn
Tomato puree ................................ 2 tblspns
Salt ............................................... to taste
Oil ..................................................... 2 tspns

### METHOD OF PREPARATION

1. Pick *rajma*, wash and soak overnight. Pressure cook in not more than two cups salted water until soft. Drain thoroughly, cool cooked *rajma* and then mash well. Reserve cooking liquor.
2. Wash green chillies, remove stem and then chop finely. Grind dry pomegranate seeds. Wash and finely chop mint leaves.
3. Mix wheat flour, soya flour, mashed *rajma*, red chilli powder, chopped green chillies, dry pomegranate powder, chopped mint leaves, tomato puree and salt to taste.
4. Add reserved cooking liquor, if required and knead into soft and pliable dough. Leave the dough covered with a moist cloth for fifteen minutes.
5. Divide into eight to ten equal portions, form them into balls (*pedas*).
6. Roll our each portion into five to six inches sized discs.
7. Brush a little oil on a hot non stick griddle(*tawa*) and place the *parantha* on it and cook on medium heat for half a minute on each side. Reduce heat and cook further till both the sides are slightly brown.
8. Serve hot with fresh skimmed milk yogurt.

### NUTRITIONAL INFORMATION

| Calories | Proteins | Fat | Carbohydrates | Fibre |
|---|---|---|---|---|
| 165 | 8 | 4.6 | 24. 9 | 1. 1 |

The griddle (*Tawa*) is a very common equipment used in Indian kitchens. Studies have shown that using of iron *kadai* and *tawa* helps to increase the iron content of the food. Hence it is advisable to make use of iron *tawa* and *kadai* for cooking.

# SALSA

## *Fresca*

### INGREDIENTS

Tomatoes ........................ 4 medium sized
Onion.............................. 1 medium sized
Jalapeno peppers .......................................... 2
Lemon......................................................... ½
Olive oil .................................... 2 tspns
Vinegar .............................................. 1 tspn
Salt.............................................. ½ tspn
Oregano(dried) ............................ ½ tspn
Fresh coriander leaves ................... ¼ cup

### METHOD OF PREPARATION

1. Wash and remove eye of the tomatoes, make a cross slit on the bottom side and immerse in boiling water for half a minute.
2. Drain the tomatoes, peel, deseed and chop them roughly.
3. Peel onion and chop as fine as possible. Wash and finely chop jalapeno peppers.
4. Squeeze the lemon, strain and keep the juice.
5. In a medium size bowl, combine tomatoes, onion and chilli.
6. Add the olive oil, vinegar, lemon juice and salt. Crush the oregano and add.
7. Mix well and let the sauce stand for at least two hours to blend the flavours.
8. Stir in roughly chopped coriander leaves.
9. Serve at room temperature with your choice of snacks or as a dip for your cocktails.

***Chef's Tip:***

*Red wine vinegar is recommended but you can also substitute with regular vinegar.*

### NUTRITIONAL INFORMATION

| Calories | Proteins | Fat | Carbohydrates | Fibre |
|---|---|---|---|---|
| 30 | 0. 8 | 1.1 | 5 | 0. 6 |

Oregano, mainly found in Italy and Mexico is good on salads, cheese dishes, lasagna, omelettes, spaghetti, soups and stews. Oregano like other herbs should be used in small amounts in cooking just for flavouring and seasoning. Oregano is known to have medicinal properties. It may be used to promote perspiration and thus treat cold, flu and fever. It is known to be effective against digestive disturbances such as indigestion and gas.

# RICE

When harvested from the field, rice is in the form of paddy, the kernel fully enveloped by the rice hull. After drying, the first stage in the refining process is the removal of the hull, which yields brown rice. This is 'hand-pounded rice'. If abrasive milling further processes this rice, the brown layer is removed to give the white rice we usually eat. The separated brown layer is known as 'rice bran'. Rice bran is a very rich source of fiber (4.3%). Milled rice or white rice on the other hand has trace amount of fibre (0.2%). Rice bran is light tan colour and possesses a relatively bland flavour with a nutty, toasted overtone.

Parboiling is one of the best ways of processing rice. Parboiling means soaking paddy in water for a period of one to three days, steaming once or twice and then drying and milling. This process implies the cooking of the grain with the husk. There are many advantages of cooking the rice in this manner. There is improved nutrient availability, decreased susceptibility to insect attack during storage, lower rate of washing and cooking losses, more swelling when cooked to the desired softness, improved digestibility with high protein efficiency ratio and stabilization of the oil content of the bran. Due to the nature of this process, nutrients present in the other layers seep into the grain, thus preventing losses during milling. Normally parboiled rice is distinguished from white rice by its yellowish brown colour. This rice is used instead of white rice mostly in southern parts of our country. Parboiled rice make excellent idlis too. Puffed rice (*murmura*) and rice flakes (*poha*) are other products of rice. They are used to make both savoury and sweet preparation.

**Nutritive value:**

Carbohydrate: 80% of rice grain is starch. Starches are completely digested from the intestine. Protein content of rice is only 7%. The amount of rice consumption is usually large and hence the amount of protein obtained is considerable. The total amount of protein in rice is lower than that of wheat. However protein (which is made up of amino acids) in rice, even after milling, is better in amino acid content than that in whole wheat. Rice lacks two amino acids, which are essential for the body i.e. lysine and threonine. But fortunately pulses are rich in these two amino acids. A diet, which is made up of all these essential amino acids is therefore more nutritious. In other words preparations like rice-*dal*, *idli*, *dosas* fall under highly nutritious category.

Vitamins: Like all other cereals, rice has negligible amount of fat-soluble vitamins. On the other hand, rice has fair amount of water-soluble B complex vitamins. Fat is present in small amount and this too is removed during milling.

**The right way of storing, washing and cooking rice:**

* A lot of people store rice. To prevent it from insect invasion, many people use mercury tablets or boric powder. This should be discouraged, instead try dried *neem* leaves or their commercially available products for storage.
* Rice should be washed in a little water only once or twice to clean dirt or other matter. The process of washing has a serious effect on its nutrient content. The losses of thiamin, riboflavin and niacin during washing are about 20-40%, 10-30% and 15-25% respectively.
* While cooking about two to two and a half parts of water to one part of rice will be enough. Newly harvested rice may need slightly less amount of water. In this way the grains will absorb all the water and no nutrients will be lost.

# MAKKAI PALAK

*Pulao*

## INGREDIENTS

| | | | |
|---|---|---|---|
| Basmati rice | 1 ¼ cups | Cloves | 2 |
| Spinach | 2 medium sized bundles | Pepper corns | 5 |
| Frozen corn kernels | ¾ cup | Green cardamom | 2 |
| Ginger | 1 inch knob | Black cardamom | 2 |
| Garlic | 4-6 cloves | Cinnamon | 1 inch piece |
| Green chillies | 2-3 | Mace | 1 blade |
| Oil | 1 ½ tspns | Lemon juice | 1 tblspn |
| Cumin seeds | 1 tspn | Salt | to taste |
| Bay leaf | 1 | | |

## METHOD OF PREPARATION

1. Pick and wash basmati rice in plenty of water and then soak in sufficient water for half an hour.
2. Clean and thoroughly wash and chop spinach. Thaw frozen corn kernels till they are soft.
3. Peel, wash, and finely chop ginger and garlic. Wash green chillies, remove stem and then slit them into two.
4. Heat oil in a non-stick pan, add cumin seeds and when they start to change colour, add bay leaf, cloves, pepper corns, green cardamom, black cardamom, cinnamon and mace. Stir-fry briefly.
5. Add chopped ginger, garlic and slit green chillies. Cook on medium heat for a minute.
6. Add corn kernels and continue cooking for two to three minutes. Drain and add basmati rice, stir gently for about a minute.
7. Add two and a half cup of water, add salt to taste. Bring to a boil, add chopped spinach and mix well. Cook on high heat, stirring gently but continuously.
8. When water is almost absorbed, add lemon juice and lower the heat. Cover the pan and continue cooking for about five to seven minutes or till the rice is completely cooked.

### NUTRITIONAL INFORMATION

| Calories | Proteins | Fat | Carbohydrates | Fibre |
|---|---|---|---|---|
| 165 | 3. 4 | 2.2 | 32. 2 | 0. 5 |

Cardamom, a common Indian mouth freshner, is also known to be one of the best and safest digestive stimulants. It treats upset stomachs, enuresis (involuntary urination), spermatorrhea, indigestion and gas. This herb is an excellent warming, antimucus stimulant to add to lung tonics.

# THREE AROMA
## *Vegetable Rice*

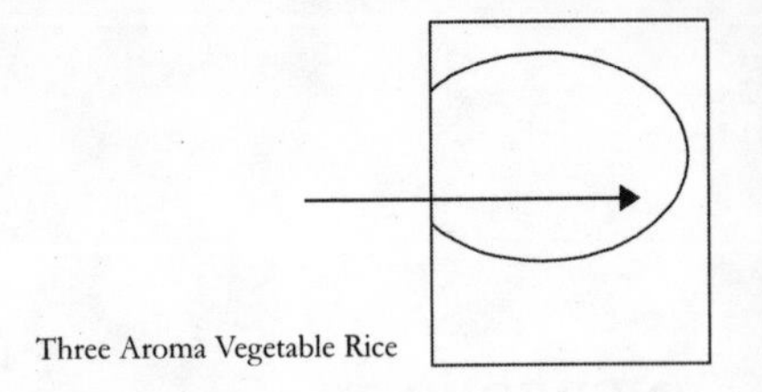

Three Aroma Vegetable Rice

### INGREDIENTS

| | |
|---|---|
| Rice | 1 ½ cups |
| Salt | to taste |
| Carrots | 2 medium sized |
| Lemon grass | 2 inch stalk |
| Cauliflower | ¼ small sized |
| Cabbage | ¼ small sized |
| Spinach | 12-16 |
| Cornflour | 1 ½ tblspns |
| Star anise | 2 |
| Shelled green peas | ½ cup |
| Crushed black pepper | 1 tblspn |
| Soya sauce | 1 tblspn |
| Sesame oil | 1 tspn |

### METHOD OF PREPARATION

1. Pick and wash rice in plenty of water and then soak for about half an hour. Drain well.
2. Boil rice in salted boiling water until completely cooked. Drain and keep warm.
3. Wash, peel and cut carrots into half cm cubes. Wash lemon grass stalk.
4. Separate cauliflower into small florets and wash them. Soak them in warm salted water and keep aside.
5. Cut cabbage into half cm. chunks. Clean, wash and trim spinach leaves.
6. Dissolve corn flour in half cup water.
7. Take three cups of water in a pan, add lemon grass, star anise and carrots and bring it to a boil. Continue to cook in boiling water for three minutes, reduce heat and add green peas and cauliflower florets.
8. Simmer till green peas and carrots are just done. Stir in cabbage and spinach leaves. Season with salt and crushed pepper corn.
9. Add soya sauce, bring it to a boil and stir in cornstarch dissolved in water while stirring continuously. Simmer for half a minute. Arrange rice in a large service bowl and pour cooked vegetables over the rice and sprinkle sesame oil on top.
10. Serve immediately.

### NUTRITIONAL INFORMATION

| Calories | Proteins | Fat | Carbohydrates | Fibre |
|---|---|---|---|---|
| 220 | 5.7 | 1. 5 | 48. 3 | 1. 3 |

A lot of vegetables are used in this recipe. Trimming is essential for removal of decayed or inedible parts. Often parts of foods are discarded for reason of palatability, even if the part is edible. Certain kind of trimming of fruits and vegetables can significantly reduce the micronutrient, which tends to be more concentrated in a thin layer right under the skin rather than in the inner parts of many fruits and vegetables. Also the dark outer leaves of vegetables such as lettuce, broccoli and celery are higher in micronutrients than are other parts of the vegetables.

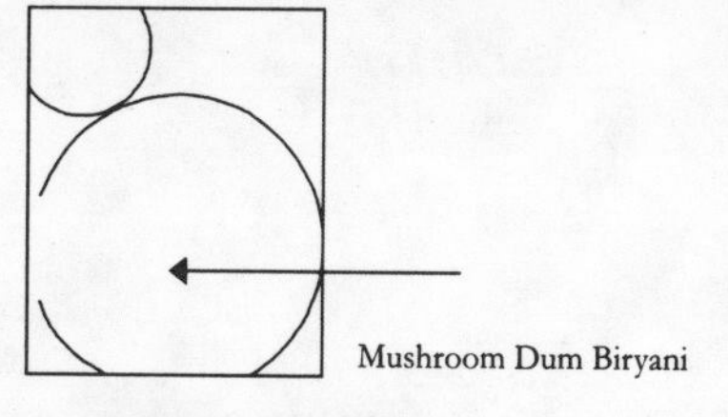
Mushroom Dum Biryani

# MUSHROOM DUM

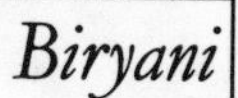
*Biryani*

## INGREDIENTS

Fresh button mushrooms .............. 15-20 medium sized
Basmati rice .............................. 1½ cups
Onions .............................. 2 medium sized
Ginger .............................. 1 inch knob
Garlic .............................. 5 cloves
Fresh coriander leaves .................... ¼ cup
Fresh mint leaves .......................... ¼ cup
Tomatoes .......................... 2 medium sized
Skimmed milk yogurt .................... ½ cup
Saffron .......................... a generous pinch
Skimmed milk .............................. ¼ cup
Bay leaf .............................................. 1
Cloves .............................................. 4
Green cardamoms .................................. 2
Black cardamoms .................................. 2
Cinnamon .............................. 1 inch piece
Mace .............................................. 1 blade
Salt .............................................. to taste
Oil .............................................. 2 tspns
Red chilli powder .......................... 2 tspns
Coriander powder .......................... 1 tblspns
Crushed peppercorn ...................... ½ tblspn
Cumin powder .............................. ½ tspn
Turmeric powder .......................... ½ tspn
*Garam masala* powder .................... ½ tspn
*Kewra* water (optional) ................ 4-5 drops

## METHOD OF PREPARATION

1. Scrub and wash mushrooms, drain and cut into quarters.
2. Pick and wash basmati rice in plenty of water and soak in sufficient water for half an hour.
3. Peel and finely slice onions. Peel ginger, garlic and grind together to a fine paste. Clean, wash and finely chop fresh coriander and mint leaves.
4. Wash tomatoes and make a puree in a blender. Whisk the skimmed milk yogurt and keep. Soak the saffron in one fourth cup warm skimmed milk.
5. Boil three to four cups water in a thick bottomed vessel, add bay leaf, cloves, green cardamoms, black cardamoms, cinnamon, mace and one teaspoon salt. When the water starts boiling rapidly, drain the soaked basmati rice and add.
6. Cook for eight to ten minutes, stirring frequently or until the rice is three fourth done. Drain in a colander.
7. Heat oil in a non stick pan, add sliced onions and stir-fry over high heat for two to three minutes or until the onion turns translucent. Add ginger-garlic paste and cook briefly.
8. Add red chilli powder, coriander powder, crushed peppercorn, cumin powder and turmeric powder. Stir-fry briefly and add the pureed tomatoes.
9. Continue cooking over high heat for another two to three minutes, stirring continuously or until *masala* is fairly thick.

10. Add the whisked skimmed milk yogurt, *garam masala* powder and half the quantity of chopped fresh coriander and mint leaves. Stir well and cook for two minutes more.
11. Add the quartered button mushrooms and salt to taste. Stir-fry over high heat for two to three minutes and remove from heat.
12. Arrange the cooked rice and mushroom *masala* in alternate layers in an oven proof dish (or Biryani *handi*), sprinkling the chopped fresh coriander and mint leaves, *kewra* water and the skimmed milk with saffron. Ensure that the topmost layer is of rice.
13. Cover the assembled biryani with a tight fitting lid and seal the edges with kneaded *atta* dough (if required).
14. Keep the sealed dish on a medium hot *tawa* and leave for ten to fifteen minutes. You can also place a few burning charcoal on the lid. Alternately, leave the sealed dish in a pre-heated oven for ten to fifteen minutes.
15. Break the seal and open the biryani, just before serving.

**NUTRITIONAL INFORMATION**

| Calories | Proteins | Fat | Carbohydrates | Fibre |
|---|---|---|---|---|
| 205 | 5. 3 | 4.2 | 36. 3 | 0. 4 |

Cloves are aromatic and are effective stimulants for the lungs and stomach. They work against cold and are good disinfectants for teeth. Cloves are rich in iron and manganese. Manganese though required in small amount, has important functions to perform in the body. It is a component of many enzymes. Its deficiency can lead to abnormality in skeletal bone mineralisation.

# TASTY PROTEIN

*Pulao*

## INGREDIENTS

Basmati rice ................................ 1 ¼ cups
Onion ................................ 1 medium sized
Ginger ............................ 1 one inch knob
Tomatoes ......................... 2 medium sized
Fresh coriander leaves .................... ¼ cup
Soya chunks ................................ 1 ½ cups
Cumin seeds ...................................... 1 tspn
Oil ............................................. 1 ½ tspns
Coriander powder .......................... 2 tspns
Turmeric powder ............................. 1 tspn
Red chilli powder ............................ 1 tspn
*Garam masala* powder ...................... 1 tspn
Salt ................................................ to taste

## METHOD OF PREPARATION

1. Pick and wash basmati rice in plenty of water and soak in sufficient water for half an hour.
2. Peel and chop onion and ginger. Wash and chop tomatoes. Clean, wash and finely chop fresh coriander leaves.
3. Soak soya chunks in luke-warm water for fifteen minutes. Squeeze to remove excess water and cut each piece into two.
4. Heat oil in a thick-bottomed pan, add cumin seeds and let them crackle. Add chopped onion and sauté for two minutes. Cook on medium heat, stirring continuously till onions turns brown.
5. Add coriander powder, turmeric powder, red chilli powder and chopped tomatoes. Continue cooking on medium heat for three to four minutes or until tomatoes are cooked.
6. Add soya chunks, basmati rice and chopped fresh coriander leaves and stir gently for a minute. Stir in three cups of water, *garam masala* powder, salt to taste and bring it to a boil.
7. Reduce the heat, cover the pan and simmer till all the water has been absorbed and rice is cooked. Serve hot.

### NUTRITIONAL INFORMATION

| Calories | Proteins | Fat | Carbohydrates | Fibre |
|---|---|---|---|---|
| 195 | 10. 4 | 2 | 27. 9 | 0. 4 |

Soya flour can be processed and extruded to give textured chunks, called protein isolates or meat alternatives. These chunks when soaked and cooked appear remarkably like meat. Such products are not only less costly than meat but score more even on health ground. They have no cholesterol, no saturated fat. This vegetable source of protein is both high in quality and quantity.

# SPROUTED MOONG

## *Khichdi*

### INGREDIENTS

Rice ........................................ 1 cup
Carrots ........................ 2 medium sized
Cauliflower ....... 4-6 medium sized florets
Green chillies .................................. 3-4
Pure *Ghee* ...................................... 1 tspn
Cumin seeds .................................. 1 tspn
Cinnamon ............................ 1 inch stick
Turmeric powder ........................ ½ tspn
Crushed Pepper corn ................. ½ tblspn
Salt ................................................ to taste
Sprouted Green gram
(whole *moong*) ........................... 1 ½ cups

### METHOD OF PREPARATION

1. Pick and wash rice in plenty of water and soak in sufficient water for half an hour. Wash, peel and cut carrots into one inch sized pieces.
2. Wash and cut cauliflower into small florets. Wash green chillies remove stem and slit then into two.
3. Heat ghee in a non stick pan and add cumin seeds. Stir-fry over high heat till they start changing color.
4. Add cinnamon stick, turmeric powder, crushed pepper corn and slit green chillies and stir-fry for a while. Add the cut carrots and cauliflower and mix well.
5. Drain and add the soaked rice and salt to taste, stir briefly and add two and half cups of water.
6. Bring the rice to a rapid boil, add the sprouted moong, reduce heat and simmer for fifteen to twenty minutes, stirring frequently or until the rice is lightly mashed and completely cooked.

### NUTRITIONAL INFORMATION

| Calories | Proteins | Fat | Carbohydrates | Fibre |
|---|---|---|---|---|
| 180 | 6. 5 | 1. 5 | 35. 6 | 1. 3 |

*Ghee* is highly valued in ancient medicine as a rejuvenative food. According to Ayurveda, *ghee* is cool, light and oily. *Ghee* aids the digestion and absorbtion of other nutrients. Home made *ghee* is valued more for its taste, aroma and medicinal properties. However *ghee*, either homemade or purchased from the market gives 9 calories/ gm or 45 calories/ tspn. It is rich in vitamin A but has high saturated fat and is not advised for patients who are suffering from heart diseases or those who are on low calorie diet.

# MURGH KHEEMA

*Pulao*

**INGREDIENTS**

Basmati rice .................................. 1¼ cup
Ginger .................................. 1 inch knob
Garlic .......................................... 6-8 cloves
Chicken mince ............................ 250 gms
Red chilli powder ............................ 1 tspn
Coriander powder ...................... 1 tblspn
Lemon juice ............................... 1 tblspn
Salt ............................................ to taste
Green chillies ................................... 4-6
Onion .............................. 1 medium sized
Tomatoes ........................ 2 medium sized
Fresh coriander leaves .................... ¼ cup
Fresh mint leaves .......................... ¼ cup
Oil ............................................... 1½ tspn
Cumin seeds .................................. 1 tspn
Bay leaf ................................................ 1
Pepper corns ...................................... 4-5
Cloves ................................................... 2
Green cardamoms ................................ 2
Cinnamon ............................ 1- inch piece

**METHOD OF PREPARATION**

1. Pick and wash basmati rice in plenty of water and soak rice in sufficient water for half an hour. Peel and grind ginger and garlic to a fine paste.
2. Mix chicken mince with ginger garlic paste, red chilli powder, coriander powder, lemon juice and salt to taste. Mix well and refrigerate until required.
3. Wash green chillies, remove stem and finely chop. Peel and finely slice onion. Wash and finely chop tomatoes. Clean, wash and finely chop green coriander and mint leaves.
4. Heat oil in a non stick pan, add cumin seeds and stir-fry till they start changing colour. Add bay leaf, pepper corns, cloves, green cardamom, cinnamon and chopped green chillies. Add sliced onion and sauté on high heat until the onion turns translucent.
5. Stir briefly and add the marinated chicken mince. Cook on high heat for two to three minutes, stirring continuously.
6. Add chopped tomatoes, green coriander and mint leaves and continue cooking for three to four minutes more. Drain and add the soaked basmati rice and salt to taste, mix well.
7. Add two and half cups water (preferably hot). Add salt and mix well. Bring to a boil and cook on high heat stirring gently but frequently till the water is almost absorbed.
8. Reduce the heat, cover the pan with a tight fitting lid and cook for another three to five minutes or till the rice is done.

**NUTRITIONAL INFORMATION**

| Calories | Proteins | Fat | Carbohydrates | Fibre |
|---|---|---|---|---|
| 255 | 18. 6 | 5.2 | 31. 9 | 0. 6 |

Herbs and spices are commonly used in Indian preparations. These are accessory foods mainly used for flavouring. Some of these spices are rich in iron, trace metal and potassium. These spices also contain several pharmacologically active substances like choline, biogenic cumins, etc. They also have medicinal properties extensively used in Ayurvedic medicines.

# DESSERTS

In any festive meal, the dessert is equally or more important than any other component of the meal. There is a lot of difference between Indian sweets and western desserts. One basic difference is that Indian desserts or sweets can be or are served along with the meal where as western desserts are served after the meal.

Traditionally, western desserts unlike Indian sweets are mostly made with refined flour, fat (margarine, butter, cream) and sugar. Products like cakes, cookies, pastries, puddings are calorie dense with fat content. If eggs are added they will give proteins. Commercial desserts have more calories as compared to home made products.

A healthy substitute to these desserts is fruit based desserts, which can be not only low in calories but also high in fibre, and packed with Vitamins and minerals. Fresh fruits can be poached, broiled or made into compote. It is best to use fresh fruits but if canned fruits are to be used, ensure that canned fruits are packed in their own juices instead of sugar syrup.

A small portion of pastry can give anywhere between 200-350 calories whereas a generous helping of Steamed fruit pudding (see recipe in dessert section) gives 160 calories and 1.2 grams of fiber and is packed with minerals and Vitamins.

Do note that desserts given in this section are fruits based. Fresh fruits are used in various combinations. They are simple to prepare and are low in calories, high in fiber, Vitamins and minerals. All desserts mentioned here can be eaten by young and old, weight conscious people or diabetics (when made with very little or without sweetening) or even heart patients.

# PEACH
## *Mousse*

**INGREDIENTS**

Ripe Peaches .................... 8-10 (250 gms)
Skimmed milk yogurt .................... ¼ cup
Egg white .................................. of 3 eggs
Corn flour .................................... 2 tblspns
Honey ........................................... 4 tblspns

**METHOD OF PREPARATION**

1. Peel, halve and remove stone from peaches. Slice peaches and keep a few slices aside for garnish.
2. Whisk egg whites lightly. Mix sliced peaches, egg white, yogurt, honey and corn flour and then put in a blender to puree.
3. Pour into a non-stick pan and cook on low heat, stirring continuously for eight to ten minutes or till it is thick and smooth.
4. Pour into individual serving bowls and chill in the refrigerator for about an hour.
5. Garnish with the remaining peach slices and serve immediately.

**NUTRITIONAL INFORMATION**

| Calories | Proteins | Fat | Carbohydrates | Fibre |
|---|---|---|---|---|
| 100 | 3. 6 | 1 | 19. 4 | 0. 7 |

Yogurt is a fermented milk product made from milk. Yogurt contains all the food value of the milk from which it is made. Yogurt is made by the bacteria which clot the milk. Yogurt is not exceptionally low in calories unless it is made from skimmed milk and is unsweetened. One cup of this kind of yogurt would give 90-100 cals and 8 gms. of protein. One cup sweetened yogurt can give as much as 260 cals and still only 8 gms. of protein.

# PEAR
## *Paradise*

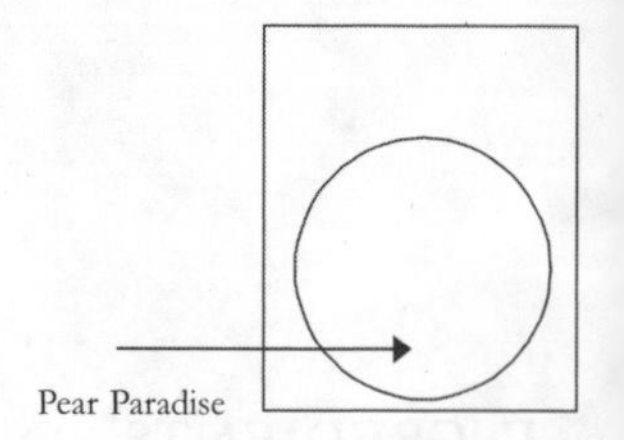
Pear Paradise

### INGREDIENTS

Pears ........................................ 4 large sized
Lemon juice .................................. 1 tblspn
Orange rind .................................. 1 tblspn
Pistachio nuts ........................................ 6-8
Unsweetened Mango pulp ............. ½ cup
Fresh orange juice ............................ 1 cup
Sherry (optional) .......................... 4 tblspns

### METHOD OF PREPARATION

1. Wash, peel and halve pears. Remove seeds, apply lemon juice and keep aside.
2. Cut orange rind into thin strips. Soak the pistachios in hot water for five minutes. Drain, peel and slice.
3. Arrange pears with the cut side facing down in a medium sized oven-proof ceramic or glass dish. Mix unsweetened mango pulp, orange rind, fresh orange juice sherry and pour on the arranged pears.
4. Bake in a preheated oven at 180 degrees Celsius for thirty minutes. Alternately cook in a microwave oven on HIGH mode for five minutes.
5. Garnish with sliced pistachios and serve warm. You may also serve this chilled, if desired.

**Chef's Tip:**

*You can use the pear peel in your regular chutney and make it more tasty and nutritious.*

### NUTRITIONAL INFORMATION

| Calories | Proteins | Fat | Carbohydrates | Fibre |
|---|---|---|---|---|
| 100 | 1. 5 | 2 | 18. 2 | 1. 3 |

It should be noted that in this dish Pistachio nuts are used only for garnishing, which do not affect its caloric content to any great extent. Pistachios are high in fat (53%) and calories (650/100 gms.). People on a low calorie diet or those suffering from heart diseases, should avoid eating nuts and dry fruits. However if this dish is prepared for kids, then the amount of pistachios can be increased since they also have a good amount of other micro-nutrients, protein (20%) calcium, phosphorous and iron.

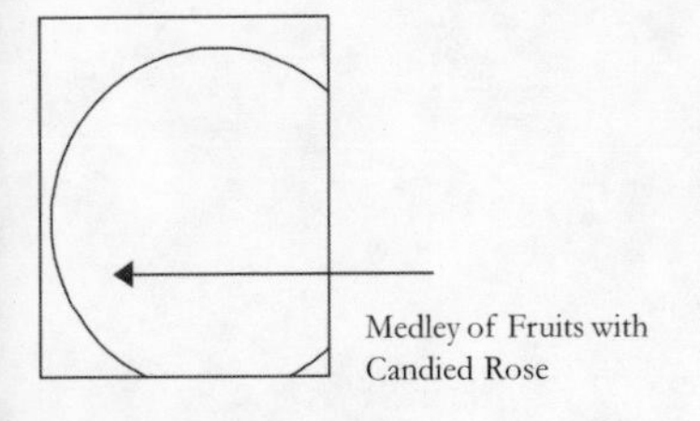

Medley of Fruits with Candied Rose

# MEDLEY OF FRUITS
## *with Candied Rose*

### INGREDIENTS

Water melon ................... ¼ medium sized
Pineapple ........................ ¼ medium sized
Apples ............................. 2 medium sized
Lemon juice ..................................... 1 tspn
Pomegranate ................... ½ medium sized
Bananas .................................................. 1
Orange ..................................................... 1
Sweet lime ................................................ 1
Chikoo ..................................................... 1
Candied rose petals (*Gulkand*) ... 2 tblspns
Fresh orange or sweet limejuice ...... 1 cup

### METHOD OF PREPARATION

1. Scoop out watermelon into small balls, using a Parisienne scoop. Scoop out pineapple also into small balls.
2. Scoop apples into small sized balls and sprinkle with lemon juice and mix well.
3. Peel pomegranate and separate the pomegranate pearls. Peel and slice the banana into six to eight pieces.
4. Peel orange, deseed, remove the white pith and cut the segments into two.
5. Peel sweet lime, deseed, remove the white pith and cut the segments into two. Peel, remove seeds and cut chikoo into thin wedges.
6. Mix candied rose petals (*gulkand*) with fresh orange juice or fresh sweet lime juice.
7. Arrange the fruits in a serving plate decoratively and refrigerate.
8. Just before serving lace candied rose petal and fresh juice mixture on to the arranged fruits. Serve immediately.

**Chef's Tip:**

*Instead of making scoops out of fruits, you can also prepare this dessert by cutting the fruits into any shape.*

### NUTRITIONAL INFORMATION

| Calories | Proteins | Fat | Carbohydrates | Fibre |
|---|---|---|---|---|
| 175 | 1. 5 | 8 | 39. 6 | 2. 1 |

Pomegranate, like other fruits is an excellent source of minerals and micronutrients. This dish is rich in all minerals like phosphorous, potassium, manganese and magnesium, to name a few. Magnesium activates about 100 enzymes in our body and helps nerve and muscle functions. It has been discovered that pomegranate contains a unique fatty acid called punicic acid, believed to give the fruit its healing powers to combat ageing. Researchers also discovered that pomegranate has chemicals that fight heart diseases and cancer.

# ORANGE RICE

*Pudding*

**INGREDIENTS**

Rice ........................................ 1/3 cup
Raisins ........................................ ½ cup
Seedless dates ........................................ 6-8
Orange rind ........................................ 1 tspn
Skimmed milk ........................................ 2 cups
Honey ........................................ 1½ tblspns
Vanilla essence ........................................ ¼ tspn
Fresh orange juice ........................................ ½ cup

**METHOD OF PREPARATION**

1. Pick, wash and soak rice in sufficient water for half an hour. Soak raisins in water for fifteen minutes. Squeeze out excess water. Chop dates roughly. Finely shred orange rind. Preheat the oven to 160 degree Celsius.
2. Boil milk in a non-stick saucepan. Drain and add rice to the boiling milk, reduce heat and cook, stirring continuously till the rice is soft and the milk is completely absorbed.
3. Remove from heat and cool to room temperature. Combine cooked rice with honey, raisins, vanilla essence, chopped dates, shredded orange rind and fresh orange juice.
4. Pour into a medium sized ceramic or glass ovenproof dish. Bake the pudding in the preheated oven at 160 degrees Celsius for fifteen minutes.
5. Serve warm or chilled.

**NUTRITIONAL INFORMATION**

| Calories | Proteins | Fat | Carbohydrates | Fibre |
| --- | --- | --- | --- | --- |
| 125 | 3. 7 | 0.2 | 27. 3 | 0. 5 |

Milk has always been considered an ideal food for infants and children and a good supplementary food for adults. Milk should find a place in any balanced diet particularly in a vegetarian diet, to provide some good quality protein, sufficient calcium and riboflavin, which are difficult to obtain in adequate quantities solely from plant foods. An adult diet should have at least 150-200 mls. of milk a day while children, pregnant and lactating mothers should receive around 250-400 mls. (2 cups) of milk a day. When whey is separated from yogurt, do not discard the whey as it contains riboflavin (water soluble Vitamin ). Human milk has less protein when compared to cow's milk. Cow's milk has less fat compared to buffalo milk. The yellow colour of cow's milk is due to B-carotene content. Skimmed milk has no fat but other nutrients are comparable.

Calorie value of 1 cup (200 ml.) milk without sugar

| | |
| --- | --- |
| Buffalo milk | 225-250 |
| Cow milk | 120 |
| Skimmed milk | 60 |

# STRAWBERRY
## *Cheesecake*

**INGREDIENTS**

**Crust**

Bran biscuits or Digestive biscuit ..... 8-10
Margarine ..................................... 1 tblspn
Instant coffee powder...................... 1 tspn

**Filling**

Fresh Strawberries......... 12 medium sized
Skimmed milk yogurt .................. 1½ cup
Skimmed milk cottage cheese...... 1½ cup
Powdered sugar .............................. ½ cup
Gelatin .............................................. 10 gms
Lemon rind .......................... of one lemon
Vanilla essence .................................. 1 tspn
Strawberry essence ........................... 1 tspn
Egg whites .................................. of 2 eggs

**Topping**

Fresh Strawberry .......... 6-8 medium sized
Strawberry or lemon jelly ........... 1 tblspn

**METHOD OF PREPARATION**

1. Crush biscuits to coarse powder. Melt margarine. Dissolve instant coffee powder in two teaspoons boiling water, cool slightly. Combine melted margarine and dissolved coffee with the crushed biscuits.
2. Line a six inch spring form pan with butter paper. Press mixture evenly over bottom of the prepared pan. Set aside.
3. Soak the gelatin in quarter cup water. Heat the gelatin lightly on a double boiler to dissolve and keep warm. Hull strawberries and roughly chop.
4. Hang yogurt in a muslin cloth for about half an hour. Place cottage cheese and hung yogurt in blender. Process until smooth. Add the other filling ingredients except egg whites. Process just until blended, scraping sides of bowl frequently.
5. Beat the egg whites until stiff. Gently fold egg white into the strawberry mixture. Pour filling into the prepared pan. Cover and chill until set.
6. Meanwhile hull and slice strawberries. Dissolve strawberry or lemon jelly in quarter cup water, bring it to a boil and cool.
7. Decorate the top of the chilled cheesecake with sliced strawberries and brush liberally with the prepared jelly. Chill until the jelly is set.
8. Remove from the spring form pan and cut into eight wedges with a sharp knife dipped in hot water.

**Chef's Tip:**

*Spring form pan is similar to a round shallow cake tin but with a removable base.*

**NUTRITIONAL INFORMATION**

| Calories | Proteins | Fat | Carbohydrates | Fibre |
|---|---|---|---|---|
| 150 | 5.5 | 6.0 | 18.5 | 0.4 |

Strawberries, one of nature's finest gifts, are sweet, taste terrific and are exceptionally low in calories. One cup of strawberries give about 40-50 calories, about 80 mg. Vitamin C and 2.2 gms. of fibre. Strawberries, like grapes and cherries contain ellagic acid, a compound which prevents the formation of cancerous cell.

# GUR AUR BADAM

## *ki Phirni*

### INGREDIENTS

Pistachio nuts ........................................ 4-6
Almonds ............................................... 8-10
Rice ................................................... ¼ cup
Skimmed milk ................................ 3 cups
Jaggery (*Gur*) ................................ 4 tblspns
Cardamom powder ......................... ½ tspn
Rose water ........................................ 1 tspn

### METHOD OF PREPARATION

1. Soak pistachio nuts and almonds in hot water for five minutes. Drain, peel and cut pistachio nuts into slivers. Crush almonds into small bits.
2. Pick, wash and soak rice in sufficient water for thirty minutes. Drain and grind the soaked rice into fairly smooth paste. Dilute the rice paste in half cup of water and keep aside.
3. Boil milk in a non-stick saucepan, reduce heat, and add ground rice mixture. Cook on medium heat for about five minutes, stirring continuously or till the mixture thickens.
4. Add jaggery, crushed almonds and cardamom powder. Reduce heat and cook till jaggery has completely dissolved. (You may notice a little curdling of milk, ignore as it is quite common for some varieties of jaggery to have this effect on milk.) Remove from heat and stir in rose water.
5. Pour into separate serving bowls, preferably earthenware. Garnish with slivered pistachio nuts.
6. Chill it in refrigerator for an hour before serving.

### NUTRITIONAL INFORMATION

| Calories | Proteins | Fat | Carbohydrates | Fibre |
|---|---|---|---|---|
| 156 | 7.2 | 5.0 | 9.0 | 0. 3 |

Almond is a rich source of calories, proteins, zinc and manganese. It is also an excellent source of Vitamin E, second only to wheat germ. Vitamin E helps protect cells from free radical injury. Hence it serves as an anti-oxidant and may help protect against heart disease, cataracts and certain cancers. It is needed for normal growth and development.

# STEAMED FRUIT
## *Pudding*

### INGREDIENTS

Apple ................................ 1 medium sized
Chikoos ............................ 2 medium sized
Bananas ............................ 2 medium sized
Egg whites .................................. of 2 eggs
Whole wheat flour ........................... 1 cup
Baking powder .................................. 1 tspn
Cinnamon powder .......................... ½ tspn
Honey ........................................... 3 tblspns

### METHOD OF PREPARATION

1. Peel and core apple. Peel chikoos and remove seeds. Peel bananas and grind to a fine paste along with apple and chikoos.
2. Mix wheat flour with baking powder and cinnamon powder and sieve.
3. Mix fruit puree, egg white and honey with a light hand. Add wheat flour and combine well.
4. Pour into pudding mould. Cover tightly with silver foil.
5. Pre-heat oven to 190 degrees Celsius.
6. Put the pudding mould in a hot water container and place into the pre-heated oven. Bake for thirty to forty minutes or till it is set. Check by inserting a skewer into the pudding and if the skewer comes out clean then it is cooked.
7. Serve warm or chilled.

***Chef's Tip:***

*You can cook this pudding in a pressure cooker without using its whistle. Heat about one cup of water in the cooker and then place the pudding mould.*

### NUTRITIONAL INFORMATION

| Calories | Proteins | Fat | Carbohydrates | Fibre |
|---|---|---|---|---|
| 160 | 3. 2 | 0.6 | 34. 7 | 1. 2 |

Banana is considered a holy fruit. Compared to other fruits, bananas are high in calories but contain fair amount of many nutrients like potassium, phosphorus, magnesium, sulphur and copper. They also have fair amount of vitamin D and E. They are highly alkaline and used to treat gastric disorders.

To reduce sugar absorption from banana intake, it is best to eat banana that is not over-ripe.

# MEASUREMENTS

| Items | Quantity | Weight |
|---|---|---|
| Almonds | 10-12 | 12 gms |
| Asafoetida (*hing*) | 1/2 tspn | 5 gms |
| Baking powder | 1 tspn | 3 gms |
| Black gram (*urad*), split | 1 cup | 220 gms |
| Black pepper powder | 1 tspn | 3 gms |
| Cashewnuts | 10-12 | 7 gms |
| Chopped coriander leaves | 1 cup | 55 gms |
| Cloves | 20 | 1 gms |
| Coriander (*dhania*) powder | 1 tspn | 2 gms |
| | 1 tblspn | 6 gms |
| Cumin (*jeera*) powder | 1 tspn | 2 gms |
| | 1 tblspn | 6 gms |
| Egg | 1 | 63 gms |
| Flour (*atta*) | 1 cup | 115 gms |
| *Garam masala* powder | 1 tspn | 2 gms |
| Garlic | 6-8 cloves | 5 gms |
| Garlic paste | 1 tblspn | 16 gms |
| Ginger | 1 inch | 15-20 gms |
| Ginger paste | 1 tblspn | 16 gms |
| Gramflour (*besan*) | 1 tblspn | 10 gms |
| Grated coconut | 1 cup | 175 gms |
| Green chillies | 10 | 2 4 gms |
| | 5 | 11 gms |
| Green coriander leaves | 1 cup | 35 gms |
| Green peas (frozen) | 1 cup | 110 gms |
| Honey | 1 tblspn | 20 gms |
| Lemon juice | (1/2 lemon) large sized 1 tspn | 3 gms |
| Medium sized carrot | 1 | 60 gms |
| Medium sized onion | 1 | 90 gms |
| Medium sized potato . | 1 | 100 gms |
| Medium sized tomato | 1 | 100 gms |
| Mustard (*rai*) powder | 1 tspn | 2 gms |
| Oil | 1 tblspn | 13 mls |
| Pigeon Pea, split (*tur dal*) | 1 cup | 225 gms |
| Red chilli (*mirch*) powder | 1 tspn | 2 gms |
| | 1 tblspn | 5 gms |

| | | |
|---|---|---|
| Rice | 1 cup | 200 gms |
| Rice flour | 1 tspn | 3 gms |
| | 1 tblspn | 7 gms |
| | 1 cup | 115 gms |
| Salt | 1 tspn | 6 gms |
| Sugar | 1 tblspn | 14 gms |
| Tamarind pulp | 1 tspn | 6 gms |
| | 1 tblspn | 16 gms |
| Turmeric (*haldi*) powder | 1 tspn | 2 gms |
| | 1 tblspn | 7 gms |
| White pepper corns | 55-60 | 3 gms |
| Yogurt | 1 tblspn | 15 gms |